BLACK CHAMELEON

CHAMELEON

Memoirs .

Survival by Assimilation

BLACK
CHAMELEON

Memoirs

Survival by Assimilation

MONTEZ DECARLO

Aventine Press

Aventine Press
1023 4th Avenue, Suite 204
San Diego, CA 92101

ISBN: 1-59330-342-4

Acknowledgments

Many thanks to my family, friends, and everyone else who was responsible for shaping my life.

Special thanks to my wife, Teresa, who kept peeking over my shoulder, asking me "what are you doing?" Baby, this is the "report" I've been working on. I love you more than life itself.

To my kids, Trezale, Gerald, DeCarlo, Curtis, Tamela, and Litahni for giving me a purpose.

To my brother, Dante, for supporting every dream I've had.

Foreword

My older brother once told me that life is nothing more than a chronological series of circumstances, chances, and fate, and when these elements are combined, the sum of gains and losses is luck. This luck can be bad or good, but if the chances you take aren't calculated, then your luck will most likely be more bad than good.

Black Chameleon Memoirs chronicles the life of Mico Brunson, a man who was born into an adverse society and into a life that was coupled with unfortunate circumstances, calculated chances, and fluctuating fate—a man who realized early on in life that, in order to survive, he had to assimilate.

I had the opportunity to meet Mr. Brunson during a business conference in Baltimore, Maryland, where he was a keynote speaker. During his speech, I picked up on several terms and references that he used to describe his climb to prominence as one of the most successful black businessmen in American history. These terms and references led me to believe that there was something under the surface he was trying hard not to reveal. It wasn't that he didn't graduate from college; that fact was already widely known. No, there was something else, and not only did I notice it, but I simply had to know more about it.

During the meet-and-greet session, I approached him when I saw the crowd thinning out. After meeting him, I found that he and I had a lot in common, and that was the catalyst for further conversation. He appeared to feel very comfortable talking with me. Maybe it was because we were both from Detroit, or it could have been that we were both black. Whatever it was, I noticed that his style of communication changed when he talked with me. When a white man in a suit approached him and struck up conversation, his communication style changed again.

At first, I felt insulted that he thought he had to reduce the level of our conversation to Ebonics just because he was talking to me, but then I reflected on my past conversations and realized how comfortable I was speaking to other black men I met in corporate America. This type of communication among black professional men is more like loosening a tie after work or after an important meeting. It's a comfort zone that we enjoy; Mico meant no disrespect.

When our conversation resumed, I told him that in his speech I sensed something in his past he was yearning to reveal. I told him that I was an author and wanted to capture his life in print. He was apprehensive at first, but he agreed to meet me later for drinks.

From that meeting, I captured his memoirs and, with his blessings, wrote this book. It is written in first person because I didn't want to appear to be simply *telling* his story. I wanted the story to come from his words. The names of the characters and the locations have been changed to protect and preserve privacy.

A Dream Deferred

Every time I see a prizefight, the old Marlon Brando quote, "I coulda been a contender" rings in my head. It strums up old memories of my days as an amateur boxer and the day my dad wanted to teach me a lesson by dragging me to the K Street boxing gym on the Southwest side of Detroit after another schoolyard fight. I remember the car ride being somewhat long because we had to travel from the eastside. The ride to the gym was actually more torture to me than what happened when we arrived.

All the way there, my father lectured, preached, scolded, and promised to whip my ass when we got home. Of course, my side of the story wasn't important. No matter what I said, I couldn't explain why I was in trouble for fighting at school for the third time in a week.

"Boy, you must have some pent-up anger in you, but we gonna see how bad you really are," my father scolded as he whipped through the crowded city streets. "And when they finish whippin' on your ass over here, I'm goin' tear it up when we get home," he continued with a snarl.

The most disturbing part of the whole ordeal, as I remember it today, is that I wasn't scared at all. As a third grader, I felt that I could deal with anything that came my way as long as it wasn't an ass whippin' from my mom or dad. Besides, I just finished putting a whippin' on a punk bully who was terrorizing my brother and his friends. The adrenaline was still pumping in me, and all I could think about was my popularity status back at school.

As we arrived at the gym, I became more excited after seeing the little white sign on the front of the building that read "K Street Boxing." I believe my father sensed my excitement from my smirk and took the opportunity to wipe the smile off my face by smacking me on the back of my head as we made our way up the front steps. From the force of the smack, I stumbled but regained my balance before reaching the top of the stairs. I made sure that I maintained my composure, just in case one of the boxers was looking out the window.

My excitement grew more intense as we entered the gym and I heard the sounds of the punches hitting the heavy bag along with the squeaky sneakers shuffling along the floor as the boxers worked out. The smell of sweat and rubber hit me as we walked through the door, and I was in heaven. We stood there for a while, me mesmerized by watching the boxers and my father intensely looking for someone.

My father stepped away to greet a man who, at first glance, appeared to be a teenager himself, but from further observation was actually in his mid-twenties. He had a small and fit frame. He and my father shook hands and shared a few laughs together. I couldn't hear the conversation because I was too far away and the extraneous sounds throughout the gym muffled the conversation. From the cordial conversation and laughter, it appeared that they knew each other well.

My attention was suddenly diverted away from my father by a boxer hitting a speed bag. I thought the speed bag routine was the most impressive part of a boxer's workout. I wanted to get a closer look, but when I started to make my way over to the speed bag, my father grabbed the back of my neck and swung me in the direction of the boxing ring.

"Bring your butt over here," my father growled. "I got somebody I want you to meet."

We made our way toward the boxing ring. The man my father was talking with extended his hand to greet me.

"How's it going, little man? My name is Coach Stanley. Just call me Coach."

We shook hands and, just as he released my hand, a boy who looked my age, emerged from behind him.

"Your father tells me that you got a lot of energy to burn. He says you're a little fighter. Is that true?"

"Huh?" I replied.

"You like to fight?" asked the coach.

"Not really. I only fight if I have to," I said as I shifted my eyes from my father to the coach and the young boxer.

I remember thinking that this boxer standing in front of me is no different from anybody I'd ever fought with at school or on my block. He was taller than I was, but everybody was taller than I was. Height or size never really mattered to me when it came to fighting. Ironically, my father taught me that the bigger they are, the harder they fall, and I proved it time and time again. But, I guess that's why I was there.

"Well you gonna have to fight Terry today, little man."

"Why. He didn't do nuthin' to me," I said, tears swelling in my eyes. "I don't want to fight him."

"Aw, he's a little punk," balked Terry as he pushed passed me on his way to the boxing ring.

"Your mama's a punk," I immediately blasted back while almost knocking him down with a push to his back.

The coach grabbed me.

"Oh no, we fight with these in here."

He grabbed a pair of gloves off the corner of the boxing ring and gave them to my dad. My dad quickly shuffled me to the side and, as he stuffed my hands snuggly in the gloves, he gave me a look to say that he won't have to whip my butt for screwing up in school after all. This time I was about to get taught a good lesson in the ring.

"Okay, Billy bad ass, let's see what you are made of," snapped my father as he tightened the strings on my boxing gloves.

I didn't respond to my father. I didn't even look his way. I kept my eyes peeled on the boxer who was dancing around in the ring. The only thing I could think of was that this skinny kid hopping around the ring just called me a punk in front of my father and other people whom I didn't even know. That, to me, was the ultimate disrespect, and he would have to pay dearly for it. The more I thought about it, the angrier I became. When my father finished tying the strings on my gloves, I quickly darted to the ring to set the record straight. The coach grabbed me again.

"This is boxing, little man. That means no kicking, no biting, and no wrestling. You understand?"

"Let him go, Coach. I'll calm him down," said Terry as he continued to dance around the ring.

"Here, keep this in your mouth."

The coach shoved a plastic contraption in my mouth and strapped on a padded helmet.

Even as uncomfortable as all of this extra stuff was, it didn't sway me from focusing on my objective, which was to pummel the boy who just called me a punk. I entered the ring and moved in for the attack. Terry grabbed me and swung me into the ropes.

"Wait for the bell!" yelled the coach.

I'd seen my idol, Muhammad Ali, fight several times and emulated him during the schoolyard fights. All I had to do was emulate him now. This was my chance to show my father that I wasn't no punk. I wanted to make him proud, so I calmed down a bit and regained my composure.

The bell sounded and I went to work by dancing, jabbing, dodging, throwing straight rights and lefts, ducking, and counter punching. It was like I'd done it all before and it felt good. My punches were connecting at will. Terry was shocked; he didn't know how to react. He went down three times and with blood starting to trickle down his nose, I went in for the kill. I landed an overhand right that brought him to his knees. Because of his height, the overhand right landed square on his chin. The other boxers in the gym went wild. I hit him again with a left hook while he was on his knees. Hell, I was fighting and he was boxing. I was no boxer; therefore, the rules of engagement didn't apply to me.

The coach quickly jumped into the ring to protect his boxer, and I looked for my father because I wanted to see his reaction. My father's response was solemn at first, but then, he smiled and raised his fists with acceptance.

After the smoke had cleared, I found out what all the hoopla was about. Apparently, the kid I just knocked out had won the state Golden Glove championship. The coach and the other boxers were stunned that I had walked through him like butter. The coach was so excited that he begged my father to let me join the boxing club. My father agreed and, twenty fights later, I was the state's ninety-five pound Golden Glove champion.

My new amateur boxing career brought me and my father closer. Once again, his wisdom was right. He introduced me to the world of boxing because it gave me an opportunity to exert my energy in a positive way. I continued to have street fights but not as frequently as before. My street fights were usually against people who came into our neighborhood to cause trouble. The fighting at school completely stopped and my grades improved. For a brief moment, I was finally on the right track. However, just as the old adage goes, all good things must come to an end.

As an educator for the Detroit public school system, my mother was totally against boxing or any other sport, for that matter, especially if the intent was solely to use the sport to escape the perils of poverty. She wanted my brother and me to concentrate on academics and not concentrate on the physical prowess and mental conditioning required to excel in sports. She felt that the time spent learning and cultivating the skills necessary to be successful in sports would prevent us from acquiring the knowledge necessary to succeed in life. To her, sports were temporary and the knowledge gained through academia was permanent. In her world, there was no such thing as a smart jock. Besides, she was against the notion that the only thing that blacks are good at is sports and entertainment. She told my brother and me that all the world wanted to see a black man do was sing, dance, and run. Every time she saw a black athlete or entertainer on television, she would always say, "I bet there's some white folks somewhere looking at this and saying, sang nigga, dance nigga, run nigga run."

After my mother found out I was boxing, she became furious and put an abrupt end to it. Even though she only stood about four-foot-five, whatever rule she set for the household was law. Not even my father, who stood six-foot-three, could overrule her.

My father could no longer hide the fact that he was taking me to boxing training after school rather than to the park or fishing. Apparently, one of my mother's coworkers came across my name while reading the sports section of the newspaper. There had been a small blurb about the recent Golden Glove championships along with a picture of the boxing team. I remember the argument that ensued that evening between my mother and father. It was quite brutal, but when the smoke cleared, my mother came out on top once again.

I couldn't just quit boxing cold turkey. I had to a least make one last attempt at doing what I wanted to do, so I skipped school the next day after my father told me I had to stop boxing and rode my bike all the way to the gym. The plan was to get there, work out, and let everyone know I would be ready for the nationals.

The plan backfired because my father called the coach earlier to let him know that I wouldn't be training with the team anymore. Although, the coach was against dropping me from the team, he had to honor my father's request. That day, the coach let me suit up and work out, but later told me I couldn't return. I was devastated. I cried so much on the way home that I fell off my bike twice from being blinded by the tears.

My First Loss

After a while, the pain of not being able to box anymore wore off, and I was eventually back to taking my frustrations out on the bullies at school. If there was one thing I hated the most, it was a bully. These were the type of guys who were bigger than the other kids they picked on, yet they really couldn't fight. I had a small frame and was considered a cutie by most of the girls, so I was a prime candidate for being bullied. I was challenged often, and I won the challenge every time.

Eventually, word got around that I was the one pretty boy you shouldn't mess with unless you wanted to get into a real fight. It got to a point that when the bullies saw me come onto the playground, they immediately stopped messing with the other kids. They knew that I didn't only fight for myself but for the other kids as well.

My frustrations about not being able to box led to other things like skipping school and hanging around the older kids from the high school on the next block. I didn't believe in hanging around large crowds of people or gangs, because I really was a loner. I just wanted to create alliances with certain groups so that if I needed something, they would know who I was and would have my back.

There were plenty of gangs around my neighborhood such as the Jefferies Projects Boys, Pony Down, Eastsiders, and the Erol Flynns. The Erol Flynns migrated to Detroit from Chi Town. Most of them wanted me to join their gang, even though I was only ten years old, but I would always tell them no. I just wanted to remain neutral because I always felt that I would be much safer that way. I didn't want to have to worry about another gang jumping me just because I was a member of a rival gang. Using this strategy, I wound up not having beef with any gang and had protection by all.

Even with skipping school and hanging out with a few knuckleheads here and there, I managed to stay a straight-A student in school. I used to smoke pot and drink liquor with the big boys, steal candy from stores, then resell it to the kids at school, and not once did I miss a beat in school. That was, of course, until I reached the sixth grade. Things changed for me at that point.

I started hanging out with a couple of boys from my block on the regular. Tommy, Shaun, Kevin, Man Man, and I all lived within three blocks of each other but never really hung out as friends. We just played sandlot football and baseball every now and then on a vacant lot two houses down from my house. Everything was innocent among us until one day, while gathered to play our weekly game of football, Kevin decided to show us something he had found behind his house.

Kevin was the most mischievous one out of the bunch. His mother was a dopehead and his dad stayed in jail for one reason or another. He rarely showed up at school; when he did, he always had this dusty look about him, like he hadn't taken a shower in days. His brother, Jeff, was a teenager and was always in trouble with the cops. Jeff would often come to our school to threaten anybody who messed with Kevin. He was crazy and had a reputation around our neighborhood as being out of control. It was good to know he was on our side.

Tommy was the pretty boy of the bunch. He always wore nice clothes and always kept up with the latest fad. His father worked with my father at the Chrysler manufacturing plant. I met him before anyone else in the group. We were actually playmates before we started Kindergarten.

Shaun was the crazy one. He was an American Indian and had a temper that oftentimes couldn't be controlled. We never knew where he lived or anything about his parents. He just seemed to show up all the time out of nowhere. Rumors were he'd been abandoned and was living in vacant houses throughout the Eastside. We never asked him about it. Truth is, we really didn't care.

Man Man was kind of like me in many ways. He was short, quiet, and ruthless when he had to be. He lived two houses down from me with his mother and a pesky older sister name Juanita. Man Man and I often slap boxed with each other just to keep our skills sharp. His mother would not allow him to box either. So, like me, he took his frustrations out on the bullies at school.

We were a mixed bag of knuckleheads, but we weren't officially a crew. At least, not until that fateful day Kevin showed up with his newfound treasure.

"Hey guys," Kevin whispered secretively. "You guys want to see something?"

At first, we thought he wanted to show us another one of his brother's used condoms.

"Hell no," I snapped. "You not going to trick us with that nasty stuff again."

"No, no, this is something more serious than that. But you guys gotta swear that you won't tell nobody about this."

"What the hell is it?" asked Shaun.

"It's something that, if anyone found out, we can go to jail for it."

"We?" asked Tommy.

"We?" I asked.

"We my ass," snapped Man Man. "I ain't did nothing."

"Oh shit, what is it?" I snapped. "What did you steal this time?"

"I ain't stole nothin," said Kevin. "I found it."

"Okay, enough already," chimed Shaun. "What is it?"

"You guys got to promise you will never say nothin' about this to nobody."

After everyone promised not to say anything and engaged in our traditional pinky shake, Shaun agreed to show us.

He pulled a blue bulky handkerchief from his jacket pocket, unwrapped it, and revealed what he had found.

"Man, is that thing real?" I asked.

"Hell yeah, it's real," Kevin shot back. "I found it in the alley behind my house."

We were all startled and amazed at Kevin's newfound treasure, which was a shiny snub-nosed, pearl-handled thirty-eight revolver. I think we were more nervous than anything else. Most kids would have played around with it, but we didn't. Instead, we decided to make a pact with each other not to tell a soul about it. We hid the gun underneath a vacant house that we often used as our hideout and storage for all of our five-fingered specials. We also made it a rule that if we ever wanted to use it, that no one person could get it by themselves. The person who wanted to use it had to take someone else with them to get it. We were so excited after seeing the gun, we actually forgot that we'd initially come together to play football. We all just wanted to get away from the scene.

On the way home, we fantasized about what we could do with the gun.

"I bet I could get anything I want with a piece like that," Man Man grinned.

"We could rule the Eastside," Tommy added.

"I would hit an armored truck and take all the loot," chimed Kevin.

"I would only use it for protection," I added.

"Protection?" griped Shaun. "Your little ass can fight. Why would you need protection?"

"The older cats got guns. So I just want to be ready."

The next day, we met in the middle of the schoolyard, our usual meeting spot. Everyone was there, everyone except for Kevin, but that was no big deal because he was always late. The bell rang, indicating that it was time to make it to homeroom. All of us took one last glance toward the open gate to the playground before making a mad dash to the building.

Kevin was on all of our minds throughout the day. It was unlike him to miss an entire day of school because that would mean he would miss free breakfast and lunch. So when lunchtime came and there was still no sign of Kevin, we reconvened at our usual spot on the playground to discuss the situation.

We remembered that there was one other time that Kevin had disappeared for about week. It was the time his father got out of jail and found out that he had stolen money from his mother's secret hiding place and spent it on firecrackers. His father beat him so bad that, when he finally did show back up at school, we could still see the welts bulging from the back of his shirt. Bothered by Kevin's absence, we started asking some of the other kids if they'd seen him, but no one did. We had no choice but to let the rest of the day pass without knowing why Kevin never showed up.

On my way home from school, I had an eerie feeling, so I decided to stop by our secret hiding place just to see if everything was all right. Our secret hiding place was a vacant building that sat on the corner of our block. To my surprise, everything was there, the candy, the money, and the gun. I felt at ease and made my way home.

Three days passed and there was still no sign of Kevin. If I could have read the sirens in the night, they would have told the story. It turned out that Kevin was found dead in his backyard; his head caved in by a brick. The most shocking thing about his death was that his own brother Jeff turned out to be the one who killed him.

Rumor had it that Jeff was furious about something. And, according to their neighbor, Mr. Bogues, he'd heard them arguing and saw Jeff slapping Kevin around something fierce in the backyard. He said that he screamed out at Jeff to stop the ruckus and told him to hold the noise down. But Jeff cursed at him and told him to mind his business. That didn't sit well with Mr. Bogues. He said that he slipped on his shoes so that he could go outside to see what was going on and to teach Jeff some manners. But, before he got downstairs, the damage was already done, Kevin was lying in a pool of blood and Jeff was gone.

The day we got the news of Kevin's death, I remember the teachers and students walking around in a daze, wondering how it could have happened and why. We knew the reason, but didn't say anything to anyone, not even to each other. Shaun took it the worst because Kevin used to let him stay in his basement for months without telling anyone. They were the closest of the group.

I remember when the news broke; Shaun disappeared to the bathroom for what seemed like hours. I was the only one who could convince him to come out of the bathroom by telling him I would take care of it. In Shaun's eyes, I was the lion slayer and he knew if I said it, I meant it.

"Take care of it?" Shaun asked while wiping the tears and the snot away.

"Yeah, you know I will," I said. "I always do. I'll take care of it."

We hugged each other, cried a little bit more, and then got ourselves together. We left the bathroom and returned to class. Shaun didn't ask how I would take care of it. He didn't care. He just knew I would. And I did, too. I just wasn't sure what I would do.

We had to read aloud that day in Mrs. Wood's class. When it was my turn to read, I told her that I really didn't feel like reading and asked her if she could choose someone else. I was just too upset to read. I was one of her best students, so she didn't force me. Besides, the news of Kevin's death upset a lot of students, so the teachers were sensitive to our feelings that day.

Frank, the class clown, wasn't as sensitive. He was also the class bully and big for his age, much bigger than all the other students. Our paths never crossed outside of the classroom and, even though we were in the same class, we never even talked to each other. But that was about to change.

Frank had to have known about my reputation as a fighter. But maybe he thought I was vulnerable because I was in pain. I really don't know what it was that gave him the courage to say something out of the ordinary toward me, but he did, which was a mistake, especially at that moment.

"Boo hoo," Frank teased in a low tone.

"What did you say?"

He sat directly across from me so I heard him, but I asked him to repeat what he said anyway.

"Boo hoo, punk," he said again with a snicker.

Just as I wiggled out of my seat to rush him, Shaun beat me to the punch. He grabbed Frank around his throat and wouldn't let go. His grip was tight but I was able to get a couple of punches off, then acted as if I were breaking up the fight just as Mrs. Woods approached. We finally managed to peel Shaun off Frank's neck. I really wasn't trying that hard. His grip gave way mostly because of Mrs. Wood's efforts, not mine. As soon as she got Frank loose, he fell to the floor, and Shaun rushed out the door. After that day, I never saw Shaun again.

Birth of a Hustler

A year passed, and I was going to the seventh grade. Shaun was gone. Kevin was gone. Tommy wound up getting hit by a car and was paralyzed from the neck down. He couldn't walk or talk. All that was left of our little crew was Man Man and me.

We were still up to our old tricks, stealing candy and reselling it to the kids at school. Our operation had matured to a science. We had the whole Eastside of Detroit covered. If you wanted to buy candy at wholesale prices, you knew who had the merchandise. We expanded our operations to stealing bikes and mixing up the parts, then reselling them. We operated out of the same vacant building we used as our secret hiding place. It was now our headquarters. Everybody knew where to come to get the best candy, bikes, and small electrical gadgets that we lifted from the five-and-dime store.

We were making a lot of money for our age. While other kids were playing after school, we were making deals with the stick-up boys. The stick-up boys would use the bikes we stole for their get away from other capers because the bikes were quiet and could maneuver through traffic easily. They would use the bikes to pull their capers, bring them back, and pay us to switch them up. Our racket was foolproof—well, almost. As always, with success, comes greed and envy.

Tyrone Churney was a new stick-up kid from the Westside. He moved to the Eastside under the radar and quickly caught on to the game. The other stick-up kids quickly accepted him because he was a cousin of a neighborhood legend named Bow Down. Bow Down became a legend because, one time, he'd used his bike as a getaway after he robbed a bank in broad daylight. He gave the cops the slip the day he robbed the bank but, several months later, a cop recognized him riding his bike in the neighborhood and tried to arrest him.

As he fought with the cop in the middle of the street, he vowed never to be taken alive. He wrestled the cop's gun away and shot him directly in the face, killing him instantly. But before he could get to his bike, just about the whole police force had him surrounded.

As the story goes, he twirled around three times and yelled "Bow Down World! Bow Down!" and started blasting at the cops. Of course, the cops filled him full of holes before he got off his third shot, but he managed to take at least two cops with him to the afterworld.

Tyrone strutted around as if he was Bow Down himself, like he was the legend just because he was his cousin. I had a bad feeling about him from the first time I saw him. I didn't like him, nor did I trust him. But since Bow Down's brother Rick introduced him to me, I gave him the benefit of the doubt. Unfortunately, my suspicions were warranted.

I noticed him casing our headquarters for weeks. Every time we were there, he was lurking in the distance, waiting to pounce like a tiger stalking its prey. I told Rick about him but he blew it off as paranoia. The stalking went on for weeks. I even think he came into our headquarters looking for our stash while we were off at school, but he couldn't find anything.

I really wasn't worried about him finding our stash because no one could find it unless they had a money and candy-sniffing dog because we kept it hidden inside the wall just beneath the windowsill in the back of the house. This is where we conducted all of our business and someone had to know exactly where it was and exactly how to pop the window ledge to get to it. Besides, we flipped most of the bikes and candy as soon as we got them. So someone stealing our merchandise was the least of our worries. We were more concerned about the money because we had to leave it there for fear our parents or siblings would find it.

As suspected, one evening, Tyrone decided to make his move on us. Just as the last wave of stick-up boys left with their new bikes, Tyrone entered through a side window. He pulled a knife and tried to surprise us, but he only surprised Man Man because I was ready for him.

As soon as Tyrone entered the room and yelled "give it up, little niggas," I met him with the barrel of my gun, well, Kevin's gun.

"Give up what, punk?" I squelched as I pulled the hammer back on the pistol.

"Hey, everythang's cool, little man."

"Is it?" I responded, still pointing the gun with my finger firmly on the trigger.

"Yeah, just put the gun away, little man."

"I'm the one with the gun, so I call the shots. Now split, punk!"

"Okay, Okay. I'm gone!"

Tyrone dropped the knife and ran out of the back door.

I don't know what happened to him after that, but I don't recall ever seeing him again.

Rolling with the Big Boys

The word spread so fast about our operation that it drew unwanted attention. Eventually, we had to shut it down because the cops seemed to pop up more often in our neighborhood. But, by the time we shut the operation down, Man Man and I became legends in our own right. I think Rick took it the hardest because he was making a killing buying bikes from us for ten dollars a piece and reselling them for triple that amount.

"Hey, little players," Rick said to us as we were closing shop for the last time. "I got another spot you cats can set up at."

"Naw, man, we gonna cool it for a little while," I told him.

"How long is a little while?"

"Just until it cools down a little."

"What you gonna do with the leftovers?"

Rick gestured to the bikes leaning against the wall.

"Nothing," Man Man said. "You can have them all. Just give us twenty-five dollars."

"Cool. Here you go."

Ricky gave Man Man the money.

"I'll pick them up by this weekend. Just leave the back window unlatched."

Rick noticed David Brimmer walking toward us and decided he didn't need to stick around any longer. There was bad blood between them, and it was obvious that Rick didn't want to stick around to discuss their differences.

Before David (pronounced Dahveed) reached us, we had locked up for one last time and were on our way home. David was the type of hustler ever snotty-nosed kid around our neighborhood wanted to become. He was always clean and had the best-looking cars around. When he stepped out of his white-on-white Cadillac Coup Deville with the fat white walls and shiny spoke rims, he set the streets on fire.

He always had a gang of young boys around him "running errands," as they called it. As he approached, I noticed that there were a couple of young bucks sitting in the back seat of his ride. I couldn't make out their faces from the distance but they were looking in our direction so I had to assume the defensive mode, especially with our pockets full with money. I clinched my gun, which was hidden under my oversized sweatshirt.

"You young brothas closed for the day?" asked David as he strolled up to us in his white silk jumper and platinum leather sneakers.

I remember thinking to myself that this cat was sharp as hell and that someday I would roll just like him.

"Yeah, we closed," snapped Man Man.

I could sense Man Man's nervousness, so I stepped up.

"Yeah cuz, we done here."

"It's cool. What time you young bucks open up tomorrow?"

"No time. We done for good."

"For good? Man, I heard you cats were doing some big-time business over here."

"Naw, just small time," Man Man cautiously responded. "Just enough for lunch money."

"Lunch money? Man, if that's the case, then you young brothas need to step up your game. Check this out."

David pulled a wad of cash from his pockets. "How much merchandise you hustlers got left in there?"

"Three. No. Five bikes," I told him, hypnotized by the wad of money in his hands.

"And candy? How much you got left?"

"It's all in this bag." I gave him the bag.

"Damn, this heavy. Look, this the deal. I'll give you three hundred dollars for the rest of your stash. How's that?"

"How about four hundred?" I asked with confidence.

Man Man nudged me.

"Whoa, little brother, you got a little game with you, huh? I'll tell you what. I'll give you three hundred and fifty dollars for everything, including that piece under your shirt."

"It's a deal, except for my piece. This is special to me." I raised my sweatshirt so he could get a good look at it.

"Yeah, I see, a Saturday Night Special," he joked as he flipped through his wad and peeled off three hundred and fifty dollars. He started to give me the money then stopped.

"What's your name, little man?"

"Mico."

"Mico? What's that short for?"

"Nothing, just Mico."

"You got a last name?"

"Yeah, but it's not important."

"Cool. I like that. You pretty sharp for a young buck. I tell you what. I'm gonna give you this money for the rest of your stash but I want you young brothas to come check out my operation. You can make five times this amount in one day."

David handed me the money, and I quickly tucked it away without counting it.

"Five times!" Man Man gasped.

"I saw you checking out my ride, Mico. I know you like that don't you." He placed his arms around my shoulders. "You can have one better than that in no time."

He dug in his pocket for what I thought was more money, but he pulled out a gold-colored card.

"All right, check it, I am going to have my young posse swing by and pick up the bikes tomorrow. In the meantime, you two swing by my place Saturday at five, and I'll put you down with some real bread. Ya dig?"

"Doing what?" I asked before I realized how stupid a question it was.

I knew what David did and who he was. He was an ace hustler, one of the best in Detroit. He was also a notorious gangster and drug dealer. I've heard plenty of stories about him, but I was just playing stupid to throw him off. I didn't want him to see me get too excited because I knew eventually the manipulation would start. I wanted to have the upper hand, even when I knew I didn't.

"You'll find out on Saturday, little playa. If not, then I'll see you on the next corner popping candy for pennies. Here's the address."

He handed me the gold card and strolled away. You see, David didn't walk, he strolled like he didn't have a care in the world. Like the world moved for him. Actually, in his world, it did.

Man Man was so excited to finally meet David that he talked my ear off all the way home. I was excited too, but I knew I needed to stay calm and focused because what we were getting ourselves into was a different level of hustling.

"Man, you gotta keep this a secret," I said. "We can't let anybody know about this. We bout to hit the big time, so don't screw it up with your big mouth."

I looked at Man Man's face as he bounced alongside me. He didn't seem to hear a word I was saying so, to get his attention, I nudged him. The nudge was so hard that he tripped over his own feet and caught a strawberry on his arm from a nearby tree as he tried to break his fall.

"Shit, Mico! What the hell you do that for?" he cried as he examined the fresh bruise on his forearm.

"Stop being so damn excited all the time."

"Excited?"

"Yeah, you was skippin' along like a little girl. We gotta keep this to ourselves. We can't let nobody know. Nobody."

"I know. I ain't gonna tell," he squeaked as he dabbed the blood from his arm with the tail of his bright yellow t-shirt."

"You promise?"

"Yeah, I promise. You know I won't tell."

"Yeah, okay. I'll see you tomorrow. I'm sorry about the strawberry. You can get me back tomorrow."

"I will, too," Man Man responded as he disappeared into his house.

In the Beginning

That night, I couldn't sleep. It was like the night before Christmas for me. I ate all my dinner, took a bath, and went to bed early. My mother came into my room to question me about my behavior earlier that night. It wasn't like me to be so quiet during dinner. I always seemed to have something to talk about; otherwise, I'd just pick on my big brother Dontrel. And, I certainly never took baths and went to bed on time without an argument. So, in my mother's mind, something had to be wrong.

"Mico?" she called as she swung the door opened and flipped on the light.

"Yes, Momma," I replied.

"What the hell's matter with you tonight?"

"Huh? Nuthin, Momma. I'm just tired."

"Tired of what, playing in school all day? I know you did something. Believe me, it'll come out. It always does."

I started thinking to myself, *uh-oh, here it comes, one of her favorite phrases*. And, like clockwork, she said it.

"Remember, whatever you do in the dark will always come out in the light."

I knew better than to respond; if I did, it would be a long night. So I just lay in bed with my eyes forced shut. My brother was in his own bed next to mine and his back was turned to us, so she didn't bother to question him. Besides, he was always in bed on time. This night was no different. He was always right, and I was the one who was wrong, even though I made straight As and Bs in school just like he did.

As she turned the lights out and closed the door, I couldn't help but wonder how I became the bad son. Was it because I had a lot of friends and my brother didn't? Was it because my dad liked to wrestle with me because I didn't cry and would always fight back, unlike my brother? I didn't know why my mother had such disdain for me. Maybe she could see right through me. Maybe she knew what kind of person I was and what type of person I would grow to be. I guess that's why she was so tough on me. Then again, maybe she never wanted me to be there in the first place. Maybe the anger she showed toward me was some pent-up anger and hostility that she had toward my father for forcing her to take me in along with my brother. I never knew the real reason she appeared to dislike me so much, and there were times in my life that I really didn't care. I just dealt with it.

I really don't know what she and my dad had in mind when they brought me and my brother home that day in November of 1969. I was three years old and my brother was five. I don't remember much, but I do remember standing up in the back of my father's old four-door Chevrolet (which he so passionately called Momasita), waving goodbye to somebody, though I don't remember who. I probably didn't care because I didn't have a tear in my eyes. My brother, on the other hand, was crying like a baby. Maybe that was the defining moment for my mother. I was the strong one, but not the chosen one. I was just along for the ride. It was my brother who'd been selected out of the line-up of orphans to join their family, not me. I just happened to be there and just happened to be my brother's brother as the story goes.

After my mother picked my brother as the lucky child to be adopted, her dreams were shattered when the social worker told her that my brother had a sibling. After learning this, my father said he refused to take one and not the other. He said if he could feed one, he could feed us both. So they agreed to take both of us home.

We were given the last name Brunson, but my mother said that she refused to change the names that our birth mother gave to us, mine being Mico DiCala and my brother Dontrel Limone. She always said that our names were our identity and that maybe our biological mother would try to find us one day; keeping the same unique names would make it easier for her. Our mother wanted us to know the truth about our adoption early in life so that we wouldn't resent her and my father in the future.

I remember that after we arrived home from the adoption agency, life was good for a little while. We lived in a three-story house with a basement on a street lined with manicured lawns. A concrete walkway intersected the sidewalk before reaching the porch steps or the "front stoop" as we use to call it. The front door was flanked by two thin door-high picture windows donned by strategically placed curtains.

As you walked through the doorway, there was a big chair, my father's chair, just to the left and a floor model television sitting to the right below the L-shaped stairwell that led to the second floor. Owning a floor model television in the late 1960s was equivalent to owning a 60-inch television today—it was perceived as a mark of success.

The most significant rooms in the house to me were the basement, the attic, my bedroom that I shared with my brother, the bathroom with the bathtub located near the center of the floor, and the den that was adjacent to the dining room. There was the forbidden door on the second floor that led to the balcony on the back of the house that we were never allowed to open and, even though the entrance to the attic was located in my bedroom, we weren't allowed to go up there either.

Of course, just because certain areas of the house were considered off limits, doesn't mean we didn't explore them. That included my father's closet where I always came across something interesting. Like the Purple Heart I found stuffed under one of his shoe boxes. I wore it to school one day, not realizing its significance, and my kindergarten teacher squealed on me. Luckily, when my teacher called home, my father picked up. He didn't whip me about it because he had forgotten where he had put it and was happy that I'd found it. He just scolded me for messing around in his closet and then went on to tell me the story of how he got injured in WWII when the Germans attacked his unit.

I say my father's closet as if it were separated from my mother's closet. It was. Their rooms were separated also. I'm sure it wasn't always like that, but it was by the time we entered into their lives. I can't remember ever asking my parents why they slept in separate rooms. I do know that it didn't stop them from satisfying each other needs because I often caught my mother sneaking to my father's room butt naked.

Our house was located in a neighborhood that was considered middle-class during the 1960s. My mother used to tell me stories of how they were one of the first black families to move onto the block and how, after the first black families moved in, the white families started making a mass exodus to the suburbs, but not before a couple of crosses were burned in their yard. When we arrived on the scene, there was only one white family left on the block. And, as luck would have it, their son Travis was one of my best friends during preschool. But, by the time I reached first grade, he was gone. Just like the rest of the white families.

I remember overhearing my father talking about the white flight from our neighborhood to one of his best friends, Mr. Beecher. His take on it was simple and nonchalant. He didn't give a damn. In fact, he didn't care if all the white people left Detroit. His dislike for the whites was deep rooted, embedded into his psyche from being raised in a segregated town in Florida.

He used to tell us horrific stories of his face-to-face encounters with the white man. One story about when he used to run moonshine from Florida to Virginia stayed with me. He told us of the night he was stopped on a dark highway in Florida by two white cops. He was on his way back from making a moonshine drop in Virginia and had a pocket full of money. The cops who stopped him knew him well because they arrested him a year ago for assault with intent to kill a white man during a fight when he took a knife and slashed the man from his throat to his belly button because the man called him a nigger while they were digging graves in a graveyard. My father was exonerated from all charges because his lawyer was able to prove self-defense due to the fact my father was struck across his face with a shovel during the altercation.

The white community was outraged that a black man could get away with attempting to kill a white man but, by chance, my father's family was ex-slaves of the mayor's family, so he was spared. The two cops who arrested him were equally as frustrated and now that they'd stopped him again, they had a chance for vindication.

My father told us how scared he was when he recognized the cops. He told me he said a quick prayer because he knew he was about to be killed. They told him that they had been watching him for a long time and knew what he was doing on the highway at that time of night.

He didn't say a word when they dragged him out of the car, handcuffed him, and threw him in the back of their squad car. When they drove him down a dark dirt road, he knew he was dead, but he wouldn't give them the pleasure of begging for his life. He said that he was willing to take whatever they were going to dish out.

Once they got to their destination, they pulled him out of the car and gave him a light beating, stole his money, urinated on him, and told him that he had one week to leave Florida. My father heeded their warning and left Florida for Detroit to live with his brother, but not before proposing to my mother who he had met about a month earlier while she was visiting family in Florida. For years, he wondered why those cops didn't kill him that night. He eventually found out that the man who he was running the moonshine for was the great uncle of one of the cops who beat him.

These stories and many more served as entertainment around the dinner table during a time in my life when everything seemed to be perfect. My father was the rock that kept the family together. He was a firm but fair man who only used threats of beating our butts if we did something wrong. He was a tall man with a strong voice, so his threats were all it took to get us on the right path. I can only remember two times my father laid his hands on me.

There was the time when I was playing with fire and almost burned the house down by throwing a burning comb that I had waved over a lit candle into my bedroom closet. This was during one of the many Detroit blackouts. The other time my father struck me was when I lost my house key. We were latchkey kids because both my mother and father worked and after-school care was not an option in the early seventies.

The only reason he beat my butt that time was because my mother was too tired from working two jobs that day to beat me, but she wanted to make sure that I learned a lesson. The beating didn't hurt at all because my father used restraint; he really didn't want to beat me for something as simple as losing the key.

His usual method of punishment was unorthodox in that he would make us stand in a room somewhere and think about what we did to get ourselves in trouble. His favorite quote was "stop thoughting and start thinking!" I never really knew what that meant as child. But as I grew older, it made more sense.

For the short time that my father was a part of my life, I learned so much from him. He was a hustler and a survivor. It was remarkable to see him in action. As an assembly-line manager in an auto-manufacturing plant, he handled his business and got the job done, and as a hustler on the streets as a jitney cab driver, gambler, and numbers runner, he handled his business. He made sure that I saw him in action. He wanted to make sure that I would grow up to be a well-rounded man, capable of surviving in any environment.

It didn't matter what he was doing, he was always sharp when he walked out of the house. His uniform for work was always pressed and it was no different when he donned his street clothes. He felt that maintaining a clean and pressed image was important for a black man. It didn't matter if he was taking out the trash, his hair was combed, mustache trimmed, teeth brushed. He always used to say that "as a black man, we already have a strike against us. The doors of opportunity would always be closed in our faces, and we didn't need to give the white man a reason to slam those doors."

Back in the early seventies, when the pimp walk originated along with bell-bottom pants and afros, we were told to stand up straight and walk like a man and were forbidden to grow our hair longer than a brush cut. To him, keeping up with trends was as ignorant as jumping off a mountain just because the fool before you jumped. Some people used religion as a reason to live a certain way, but my father's ways weren't due to religious beliefs; they were just the values that he lived by to ensure his survival.

Toward the mid-seventies, our survival as a family was threatened by the economic downturn of the auto-manufacturing industry. My father was laid off from several industry jobs. It got so rough that I remember we used to eat pork and beans with rice at least four times a week and, as a treat on Fridays, my mother chopped up hot dogs and served them with the pork and beans. Times were rough and they didn't get any better but, through it all, my father kept a roof over our heads, clothes on our back, and food in our bellies from hustling.

He used to "run a jitney" with Momasita all day and sometimes he would let me come along so that I could experience earning an honest buck. I would help load the groceries in the car and carry them to the house for his customers. When night fell and the grocery stores closed, he would flip the script by frequenting his gambling spots and running numbers.

Times got hard and the arguments between my mother and father became more frequent. Eventually, the arguments led to fighting, but my parents never let us see them argue though, we heard everything. Our walls were thin, and we saw the results the next morning.

My mother often surfaced the next morning with a black eye, busted lip, or sometimes both. But, with her pride, she would put on her Sunday dress, her sunglasses, get us dressed, and we would go to church. Her strength through our economic ordeal was just as honorable as my father's strength. After the fights, my father would say nothing. He continued his daily routine as if nothing ever happened. My mother knew he had a bad temper and would manage to push all the wrong buttons at the wrong time. Eventually, his temper led to his demise.

On one of our routine trips to one of my father's gambling spot, a confrontation ensued between my father and a man outside. They scuffled, and it appeared that my father came out on top. As he backed away, I saw blood streaming from the belly of the man he was fighting. Another man emerged from the doorway with a gun pointed at my father. But before I got a chance to warn my father, I heard a bang. My father stopped arguing and turned to the man who shot him and said, "Okay, you got me."

I was in shock and couldn't say a word. My head was spinning so fast that I remember my mouth moving, but I don't recall any words coming out. He didn't fall immediately from the gunshot. Everybody scattered and he was able to make it back to the car. He managed to open the door and get in the car. He gazed at me for about a minute before closing his eyes and falling into a slouch. That was the only time I had ever seen my father slouch.

That day was saddest day of my life. As a twelve-year-old boy who idolized his father, I had questions that couldn't be answered. I remember vowing to my mother that I would eventually find and kill the man who killed my father. I told her that not only did I know his face, I knew who he was. The look on her face said it all. She knew I was capable of following through with my threats and that, eventually, I would. From that day forward, she started making plans to move the family away from Detroit.

Stepping Up My Game

Fortunately, my mother's plans for moving didn't take form before I met David. Saturday came quick, and Man Man and I were about to step up our hustle game. We were about to take it to another level.

When we reached the address on the card David gave us, all of my nerves seemed to go away. I had the same feeling I used to get just before stepping in the ring; the butterflies just flew away because I had to focus on taking care of business. Man Man was still nervous, and it showed. After I calmed him down, we knocked on the door. One of David's women answered the door.

"C'mon on in, little playas," David summoned from the couch.

As we entered, we saw a bunch of boys our age milling around the house. Some were counting money off in the distance and others were measuring some type of white substance on scales and putting it in different sized bags. There were young boys our age all over the house. Each of them seemed to have a job. The white substance turned out to be cocaine and heroin.

Butch, a known gangster in our neighborhood, flanked David. Butch was known all over Detroit as David's enforcer. He rarely left his side, a crazy fool with nothing to lose.

"What's happening?" I said as we made our way over to the couch.

"This is Mico and Main Man," David said, introducing us to Butch.

"Man Man," replied Man Man, correcting David.

"What kind of name is Mico?" asked Butch.

"The kind of name my mother gave me."

"You smart-assed little punk, you betta watch your mouth before I bust your punk ass," snapped Butch as he reached for my shirt.

I slipped his reach and got into my fighting stance.

"Whoa, settle down, little hustler," David snapped. "Man, you better watch out for this one. He might take your spot. He's pretty quick on the draw."

"He'd better watch his mouth and his step or you'll be drawing him a pine box."

David stood up and led us to another room. I kept my eyes trained on Butch and the other boys in the room. This was new territory for me, so I had to stay on my toes. After closing the door, David filled us in on his operation and gave us our assignments. The deal was a sweet one and seemed easy.

Our job was to deliver merchandise to different drop points, pick up the money, and bring it back to David. We would receive a hundred dollars for each trip. Hell, it would've been hard for any grownup to turn down an opportunity like this. For boys our age, it was an opportunity of a lifetime. Most of the deliveries would be scheduled before school, after school, and on the weekends.

David didn't want anyone on his crew skipping or dropping out of school. He would always say that an "ignorant nigger is a dangerous nigger and can't be trusted." He didn't want quitters on his team. He wanted winners. That was the only way he felt his empire would grow. If you dropped out of school, you were dropped from his crew. I thought it was a joke at first. But when David asked to see all of our report cards one day, I knew he was for real.

Man Man and I were making so much money with our new hustle. In a couple of months, we had enough money to buy a shiny white Cadillac just like David. It was fun to talk about, but because my father taught me the value of a dollar, I wouldn't splurge on anything. I just stuffed my mattress with all my money and, from time to time, I would slip a couple of dollars in my mother's purse without her knowing it. She would always find an extra twenty dollars here or fifty dollars there and she never caught on. At least she didn't lead me to believe she knew where the extra money was coming from. Even though, I was making a lot of money and making straight As and Bs in school, there was still tension at home.

After my father's death, the arguments between my mother and I got worse, even abusive. I believe she knew, deep inside, that I was up to something mischievous, but working two jobs, she didn't have the energy or time to try to pin me down. So every chance she had to pick an argument with me or hit me, she would. Our relationship became abusive, mentally and physically. I started to resent my father for dying because he used to be my protective buffer. When she started in on me, he used to just pick me up and put me in the car with him and we would ride all night and wouldn't come back home until she fell asleep.

Now he was gone and I didn't have that shield anymore. I had to face my mother head on. Our confrontations were brutal and, of course, I would always get the short end of the stick. There was no way in hell I would hit her back. She was crazy.

At home, there was just no peace and, with my father gone, my mother was faced with raising two boys alone. My brother wasn't the problem, he was a saint in my mother's eyes. I was the one causing my mother all the grief. Part of me just wanted to pack up and leave for good. I had enough money to make it on my own, but another part of me tried to understand her anguish, so I decided to stay and try to find peace outside of my mother's house.

I found that peace with David's crew, Young Hustlers Incorporated, YHI. We were feared and respected all over Detroit. David's elusive hustling strategy kept us from being caught by the cops or jacked by other crews. We used different houses for our meetings, never wrote anything down, and we never kept a routine, even when dropping off and picking up the goods. The cops even raided several of our locations but never found a trace of us. Our method of operation was so tight that we would know when there was a plan to raid one of our locations because we had YHI members on the police force.

After each successful drop, my status rose in the organization. My creative suggestions for setting up new drop areas and new ways to make the drops were something new to the crew. I would put together the plan for the new drops and execute them flawlessly. I was on the rise and taking Man Man along for the ride. No one could stop our flow. No one, that is, except for my mother.

Unfinished Business

The day I dreaded the most finally came. My mother told us that we were moving to Port City, North Carolina, after the school year ended. My world crumbled at the news, but I knew if I wanted to stay, all I had to do was say the word and David would make it happen. But the thought of being separated from my brother, my only bloodline in this world, weighed heavily on my decision. The only thing I could think of after hearing the news was that I had unfinished business to take care of, and I didn't have a lot of time left. I had to start planning my next move.

The day came when I had to tell David and the crew that I was moving south with my family. I really didn't know what reaction to expect, so I decided to just blurt it out at the next meeting.

"Hey, I got an announcement to make," I yelled while everyone was settling in for the meeting.

"It's not the time for announcements," Butch replied. "We have other business, so sit the fuck down."

"But this is important," I replied as I made my way to the front of the table.

"Does this have something to do with my money," snapped David.

"Kinda."

"Kinda? Well, you better start talking then."

"I gotta drop out of the crew."

"What?"

"What the hell are you talking about, Mico?" asked Man Man.

"I gotta move to North Carolina with my family."

The room started grumbling then got very silent. David just stood there looking at me for what seemed like an eternity.

"Okay, we'll discuss your options after the meeting. Now sit the fuck down," David said.

I slithered back to my seat, not knowing what was going to happen next. David didn't look happy. I don't know if he was mad at the news of me leaving or the fact that I didn't tell him first before blurting it out in front of the crew. Whatever the reason was, I knew he would tell me soon enough.

As the meeting ended and everybody passed by me, some shaking my hand and others shaking their heads, Butch brushed up against me and whispered, "Nobody leaves YHI, you know that."

"I'm not leaving YHI. I'm leaving Detroit," I responded as we gazed at each other. "Believe that."

"Believe that," snapped Butch.

David grabbed a chair, turned it backward, and sat down in front of me.

"So, you moving down south, huh?"

"Yeah, south."

"When is this supposed to happen?"

"In a couple of days."

"I'm sensing that you don't really want to leave, do you?"

"Nah, not yet."

"Then don't."

"You think I got a choice?"

David gave me a look that inferred that I knew I had a choice. All I had to do is say the word and my mother would be making that trip without me.

"You know you always have a choice, little hustla. We make our own choices. You know that."

On the surface, I thought I could make any choice I wanted but, deep down, I knew I really didn't have a choice. If I decided to stay, I knew my mother would track me down and skin me alive. Her beatings were brutal. My decision to leave really came down to whether I was willing to face the wrath of my mother. Safe to say, I wasn't. However, in the back of my mind I couldn't stop thinking about my status in the crew and how much money we were making. The money aside, I also knew I had something to take care of, and leaving gave me an opportunity to take care of it and get out of town. My father's killer had to be dealt with and, in my mind, I knew my father would not rest until I handled it.

"You're not moving tonight, so you got some business to handle," David said as he hopped out of his chair.

"Wha What?"

"Gratiot."

"Oh yeah, right, the Gratiot drop. Sorry, I almost forgot."

"No problem. Make it your last one."

"Yeah, uh, okay."

"What's with the face? What's on your mind?"

David was very good at reading people. I know he knew something else was on my mind other than making a drop. I also knew David knew the man who killed my father. I had to play my hand before the opportunity slipped by.

"It's just that I'm not ready to go yet."

"When's your mom planning on booking again?"

"On Sunday."

"I hope you saved some of that dough you made. Oh, wait, I'm sure you did because you still wearing those raggedy-assed shoes."

David looked down at my worn Chuck's and snickered.

He was right. I barely spent any of the money I made. I didn't have the desire or time. Not to mention that I didn't want to have to explain to mother how I got the money to buy new clothes. Besides, my mother provided everything we needed, a house, food, and clothes on my back, even though the clothes, for the most part, were secondhand or hand-me-downs from my brother. I just stuffed the money in my mattress and lived each day in agony with my brother as if I didn't have any money at all. My brother didn't know what I was up to. I think he suspected something, but he never said anything because he was too involved with school and other corny crap. He was in his own world.

"Yeah, you right." I chuckled as I wiggled my big toe out of the side of my shoe.

"You need me to take you shopping?"

"Naw . . . I'm cool. But . . . I do need something else from you."

"What is it, little hustla? You know I got your back."

"Some heavy shit been on my mind lately. So much that I can't sleep anymore."

"What's that? What shit? Somebody's fucking with you?

"Well kind of," I said as my mind started spinning in every direction.

"Yeah, who? C'mon, mofo, you know I ain't got no patience for riddles."

I paused for a second as I got up the nerve to tell David what I really wanted. At first, I didn't know how I should say it. But I thought the worst that could happen was that David would probably have the mofo killed himself and not give me the satisfaction of killing him.

"The punk who killed my father."

"Who . . . Isaac?"

"Isaac? Who the fuck is Isaac?"

David pulled the chair back in front of him. Just as he sat down, someone came to the door.

"D?" asked the voice through the crack of the door.

"Not now . . . in a minute," David said. "I got business"

The door closed and David directed his attention back to me.

"Isaac?" I asked again.

"Yeah, that's him.

"You know him?"

"No. But I know where he lay."

"How so?"

"My uncle lives across the alley from him. I can handle it for you."

"No. This is something I gotta do."

"How do you plan to deal with it?"

"My heater."

I took Kevin's gun out of my waistband and placed it on the table in front of David.

"Oh yeah, I forgot the little hustla was packing. That thing got any bullets?"

Just at that moment, Jeff opened the door and looked in. He saw David talking to me and quickly started to shut the door. But before he did, he gazed at the gun lying on the table in front of David. He gave me a nasty stare. It turned out that the reason Jeff killed Kevin, his own brother, was because of the gun sitting on the table in front of me.

Jeff was the recon man for YHI. His job was to stay low key and scope out new locations for us to hold our meetings. Hardly anyone knew he was part of the crew because he wasn't knee deep in the real operation. David kept him low key because his mind took a turn for the worse after Kevin's death, but since he and David grew up in the Jay Projects together, David felt obligated to keep him employed. They started out as the notorious Jay Boys but later migrated to YHI, David's brainchild.

David sensed the tension from Jeff's stare and quickly went into moderator role.

"What' up with you, J?"

"Nothin."

"Nothin? You look like you seen a ghost."

"Nothin' that I can't handle, nothin' that I won't handle," Jeff said as he closed the door.

I grabbed the gun off the table, shook hands with David, and left. I avoided running into Jeff on the way out because I didn't want anything to pop off around David. I didn't know if Jeff and David was still close.

School was about to end and my time was running out. I only had a couple of weeks left to map out my plan before moving to North Carolina. The timing for my plan would be crucial, from the timing to the route I would take, to the alibi I would use in case I was questioned, to the time we packed up the house and hit the highway. All the preparation for something as simple as pointing a gun at a man and pulling the trigger seemed excessive. But planning was something that my father instilled in me. This is what he meant when he used to say, "stop thoughting and start thinking." The hit had to happen the same day or the day before we were leaving for North Carolina. I mapped out my escape route several times and practiced my story just in case someone saw me in the area.

The week before I was to make my move seemed like the longest week in my life. My mother made it longer by complaining every day about something or scolding and beating me about every little thing. In one week, I got slapped in my mouth for spilling milk, a beating for not locking the door behind me when I came home from school, punished for picking on my brother, and beat almost half to death for stealing her wedding ring to give to a girl I liked in my class. I wanted her to have something to remember me by, but wound up getting a beating that I would never forget. After being beat half to death by my mother, I felt that I had enough of her abuse and ran away. The only place I had to go was to YHI or to my Aunt Lucy's house. I chose YHI.

As I approached the door to our new location for the week, I heard loud noises coming from the inside as if someone were fighting. When I entered, I saw Jeff standing over Man Man choking him. My instinct took over, and I immediately ran and jumped on Jeff's back, wrapping my arms around his neck.

"Get off him," I yelled as tightened my grip.

At first, the other guys who were in the room just stood around and watched Jeff pummel Man Man, but when I jumped in, they rushed to my aid before Jeff had a chance to figure out what was going on. All the guys just piled on. At first, I didn't know if they were helping Jeff or if they were helping me, so unbeknownst to anyone, I pulled my gun and fired two shots into Jeff at close range. Everyone scattered while Jeff grabbed his chest and slumped to the floor.

"I knew Kevin gave it to you, you little punk," he said before taking his last breath.

I was so angry that I wanted to pump him with more bullets but immediately came to my senses. I only had four bullets left, and I didn't want to waste them. I ran out the front door before the shock wore off and before one word was muttered. I jumped on my bike and headed for my Aunt Lucy's house.

The only thing that I could think about, as I rode my bike at lightning speed, was that I hadn't planned for what just happened and that my father would be disappointed. So I started thinking about what my story would be when the cops came after me.

When I arrived at Aunt Lucy's house, she greeted me with open arms, just as she had many times before.

"C'mon in, baby," Aunt Lucy said as she unhooked and opened the back screen door.

"Hey, Auntie," I said in a low tone.

"C'mon in and get something to eat."

Aunt Lucy always offered her guests something to eat. Food was never scarce in her house, and her hefty size was proof of it.

"Your mother got you all riled up again, baby?"

"Yes. It never ends, Auntie. I don't think it ever will."

"It will get better, baby. You'll see. When you guys move down south, all your mother's tension will be lifted. Just stick in there."

"I don't wanna go. Can I stay with you?"

"Oh, baby, I would love for you to stay with me, but I don't think your mother would allow that. Besides, you need to go with your brother and help look after her. She needs you guys now more than ever."

She placed a plateful of food in front of me.

"Here you go, baby, now put something on them bones. When you finish, you know where everything is. Take a bath and get yourself a good night's rest."

She gave me a snuggle hug, one that only she could give, and disappeared to her room for the night. My Aunt Lucy had a way of making people forget about all of their problems by feeding them good food and always making them feel loved and welcome in her home. She was my mother's sister, but they were like night and day.

Digging into the plate of food in front of me made me forget about the conflict with my mother and the conflict with Jeff. Besides, Jeff got what he deserved and my mother, well, she was my mother, and I couldn't change that.

After finishing my dinner, I had to make sure that I called my friend to get the homework assignment for the next day. It didn't matter what was going on around me, I always had to make sure that my schoolwork was in order. In my mind, finishing school was the only ticket out of my mother's house.

The next day came, and I woke up to the smell of sausage and eggs coming from my aunt's kitchen. My clothes were already pressed and hanging on the doorknob. I ate breakfast, brushed my teeth, kissed my aunt, and headed for school. On my way, the only thing I could think about was if I was going to make it on time. My mother never crossed my mind, nor did shooting Jeff. My conscience was clear, my mind was refreshed, and I was ready to face the day's new challenges.

I couldn't help but wonder if David was now looking for me for shooting a long-time friend of his. Or maybe he'd taken his anger out against me by killing Man Man. I didn't know what happened to David or Man Man nor did I care to find out. I developed the innate ability to block all the bad things that happened to me and daydream about all the good things that I wanted in my life. The only bad thing that I couldn't block was my father dying in front of me. I hoped the memory of that would be wiped out after I took care of Isaac.

After school, I returned home. Whenever I ran away from home and came back, my mother never questioned me about where I went or what I was doing. Everything would be the same as it was before I left, which was unfortunate.

"Boy, take your ass to your room and make sure you finish packing all of your clothes in those boxes and don't pack any broken shit," my mother yelped as she saw me coming through the front door.

Without a response, I followed her command. When I got to the room, my brother was already finished packing.

"You seen Man Man?" Dontrel asked.

"No. Why?"

"Juanita came over here all hysterical and asking about him. I think they already called the police."

"I was over Aunt Lucy's house."

"Yeah, right."

"I was. You can call her and ask her."

"You and Man Man don't go anywhere without each other. You know they gonna ask you have you seen him."

"So? I'll tell them the same thing I told you."

"When was the last time you seen him?"

My brother's questioning gave me an opportunity to practice my response just in case the cops asked me any questions.

"The last time I saw him was when we left school yesterday. I went to the Shopmart and Man Man went home. He said he had to get home for something. That was the last time I saw him."

"Make sure you stick to your story," Dontrel jested as he left the room.

I couldn't help but wonder if one of those bullets from my gun found Man Man. There was no way for me to find out without going back to the scene of the crime, and that was something I would never do. I checked the newspaper and watched the news but saw nothing regarding Man Man or Jeff.

We finished packing all of our stuff and it was being loaded on the moving truck. The next day, we were hitting the highway.

"Are you ready to roll, little man?" asked my Uncle Tig as I was coming down the stairs.

My mother had two brothers, Uncle Tig and Uncle Bite who were from North Carolina but lived in Detroit. They came over to help us move. After my father died, they stepped in as surrogate fathers to my brother and me.

Both of them considered themselves lovers and smooth operators. I looked up to both of them. Uncle Tig for his fast rides and fast women and Uncle Bite for his smooth talk and funny catch phrases. The day of my father's funeral, I remember my Uncle Bite sitting us on his lap and telling us that he would always be there for us, no matter what. I could talk to my uncles about anything and anyone. I often called them when my mother would blow her stack and they would calm her down.

My Uncle Bite got his nickname from telling women that he don't nibble, he bit. And, my Uncle Tig got his nickname from all the women calling him a tiger in bed. I never really knew their real names.

"Yeah, Uncle Tig, I been ready," I replied.

"Don't get down there and run those country girls crazy."

"You know I will."

My Uncle Tig laughed as he gave me a soul shake and a hug.

The only people I truly felt loved by as a child was my father, Aunt Lucy, Uncle Tig, and Uncle Bite. The only time I would hear the word love come from my mother was after a beating. She would say something like, "the only reason I whip your ass is because I love you" or "if I didn't love you, I wouldn't whip your ass."

That day, everything seemed perfect. Everybody came by the house to say their farewells and to wish us luck on our new life in the South. That night, we had a big going away party. Everybody I loved was there. My Aunt Lucy cooked all of my favorite foods. She was going to be the one I would miss the most. It always seemed when I needed someone, she was there. She never talked bad about anybody, especially my mother. Her positive attitude just seemed to rub off on everybody.

"Come here, baby," Aunt Lucy called as she saw me getting gifts, well wishes, and aimlessly bouncing from person to person.

"Yes, Auntie?"

"You know I love you very much, don't you?" She gave me the snuggle hug that only she could give.

"Yes, but I love you more."

"I want you to be good and listen to your mother. She is going to need you now more than ever. Okay?"

"Okay, I am going to miss you so much, Auntie" The tears swelled in my eyes.

"I will miss you more. You know you can come visit me anytime."

"Anytime?" I ask excitedly.

"Yes, you know you're always welcome."

"Can I come live with you?"

"Sure. Only if your mother says it's okay. But first, I want you to help her get settled in North Carolina." She gave me another snuggle hug.

"Okay."

As I kissed her on her cheek, I caught a glimpse of David's car slowly creeping down the alley behind my house. At that moment, thoughts of Man Man rushed through my mind, and I broke away from my auntie's embrace and ran toward the back gate to get David's attention. But before I reached the back gate, David was gone. Man Man stayed on my mind for the rest of the night. I had to do everything in my power not to go looking for him. I still wasn't sure if I was the reason for his disappearance. Besides, we were leaving the next day, and this chapter of my life would be behind me.

For a few hours more, I mingled with the friends and family who had come to see us off, trying to keep my mind clear and off the mission that I had to do the next day. I was convinced that the mission would certainly bring closure to the pain I'd felt ever since my dad was killed.

Later that evening, after most people left the party, I retired to my room to go over the final plan. I had mapped out my escape route from Isaac's house and, because of the information David had given me, I knew exactly when to strike. David said Isaac washed his car around eleven o'clock in the morning every Sunday while his family was at church. Most people in the neighborhood would be in church around that time, including us. However, on this particular Sunday, I had to figure out a way to get out of going. My mother didn't play around when it came to going to church. Even if we said we were sick, she would make us go and would always say that the Lord would make us well. If I were to play sick, I knew I had to be real convincing.

The next day came, and I had to put my plan in action. My brother got up on time, as usual, so I knew I could use him to get the ball rolling with my mother.

"Dontrel," I said in a weak tone.

"What, Mico?"

"Tell Momma I'm sick."

"You tell her. I'm not going to lie for you."

"I'm not lying. Feel my head."

Dontrel placed his hand on my forehead.

"It's kinda warm. How did you do that?"

"It musta been something I ate last night."

"No. I mean, how did you get your forehead to feel so warm?"

"I'm really sick."

"Yeah, right."

As he left to go tell Momma the news, I had to make sure that all my props were hidden. I tucked the jacket I used to give myself the sick sweaty look and the hot washcloth I used to make my forehead warm on the side of my bed and out of view of my mother. I knew, after my brother gave her the news, she would be up to my room with thermometer in hand. And, like clockwork, she burst through my bedroom door.

"Boy, don't play that crap today. What in the hell is wrong with you?" she asked as she vigorously shook the thermometer.

"I don't feel good," I answered weakly.

"We'll see." She shoved the thermometer in my mouth and placed her hand on my head. "You are kind of warm. Leave that thermometer in your mouth. I'll be back in a couple of minutes."

She left the room and went back downstairs to check on breakfast. I knew that I only had a couple of minutes to work my plan to perfection. The hot cloth had turned lukewarm, so I couldn't use it to run the temperature up in the thermometer. I had to use the next best thing. The sun often peered through our window in the mornings, so I had to find a good sunray to bake the end of the thermometer. Luckily, it wasn't cloudy that morning. I found a good sunray and was able to get the temperature up to one hundred and two.

My mother came back to check the thermometer. After checking it, she accepted that I must have been sick and allowed me to stay home from church. I was happy that the first part of my plan had worked. The timing and the execution was perfect. After my mother and brother left for church, I started preparing for phase two of my overall plan. My mother would be back by one o'clock, the movers would be at the house at two o'clock to make final preparations, and we would be on the highway going south by four o'clock. With butterflies in my stomach, I grabbed my gun from its hiding place and started mimicking what I thought was about to happen. After a few trial runs, I was ready to make it happen. I jumped on my bike and headed for Isaac's house.

Once I reached my destination, I noticed Isaac leaning into his car. He was there, just as David said he would be. I didn't want to waste time or give anyone a chance to notice me, so I made my move. I approached Isaac from behind and, just as he lifted his head out of the car, from point-blank range, I squeezed the trigger four times. I heard three loud bangs and a click. I immediately turned and ran from the scene. I didn't stay to see his body drop. I wanted to stay and see him take his last breath, just as I saw my dad take his last breath, but it was too risky. I knew the nosy neighbors would soon be looking out of their windows or back doors. I ran faster than I'd ever run before, jumped on my bike, and followed the path home just as planned. It all happened so fast. I never looked back.

When I got home, I took the gun apart. The gun was still hot, but I had to make sure that I completed the most crucial part of the plan—to get rid of it. I still had time to spare before my mother and brother returned from church, so I disassembled the gun and hid each piece in separate vacant houses along our street.

After my mother returned from church, we packed the rest of our things, loaded up Momasita, and headed south. The journey was long, but it gave me enough time to reflect on all the fond and not so fond memories I had of Detroit. I remember thinking about all the things I used to do with my friends, my dad, my family, and YHI. Although, the memories of me shooting someone haunted me for about an hour on the trip, I never really thought that I had killed anyone. I always thought of it as me shooting somebody because they deserved it. Because I never stayed to see my victims die, in my mind, I didn't kill anyone. They could be still alive, but I would never know it. Besides, after we crossed the state line, that chapter of my life ended and a new one began.

A New Beginning

I awoke to a sudden jerk from the car stopping and to an ungodly stench in the air. The smell was so awful that it brought tears to my eyes.

"Where are we?" I asked, holding my nose.

"We're home," replied my mother. "My home. This is where I grew up."

At that moment, people began racing toward the car and a very old man picked up the rear at a slower pace. As I glanced around, I didn't see any streetlights, no sidewalks, and no tall buildings, just woods, woods, and more woods. The people who came to the car looked much different from people I was accustomed to. They were wearing old raggedy clothes, dusty overalls, and didn't have any shoes on. I couldn't understand how they could not wear shoes and run over dirt and rocks without hurting their feet. I remember praying that this could not be our new life; that maybe we were just stopping to see family along the way.

"Get out and say hello to your cousins and grandfather," ordered my mother.

My brother and I were still trying to digest all of the new sights, sounds, and smells of our new environment. We got out of the car cautiously.

As we stepped out of the car, the smell got worse and the bugs were unbearable. There were these little flying insects that always managed to go up your nose and in your ears. There were swarms and swarms of them everywhere. I fought them off, but my brother was so terrified that he got back into the car. After surviving the initial shock of the Southern atmosphere and meeting my cousins and grandfather for the first time, we settled into what my mother called our temporary home. She bought a trailer home and placed it on land she had purchased from descendants of my great grandfather's slave master. This was the same land that my grandfather, as a sharecropper, was on the verge of losing because of one bad farming season. My mother was very proud of the fact that she moved away, got an education, and was able to help the family in their time of need by buying the land her father had worked so hard to keep as a sharecropper.

My mother never wanted to go back home to the deep South but, because of our circumstances, she swallowed her pride and was determined to do whatever she had to do to get back on her feet. After our father died, she often swallowed her pride and did whatever she had to do to keep a roof over heads, food in our mouths, and clothes on our backs. This detour to Logan, North Carolina, was just another method she took to ensure our survival. After a while, it didn't seem so bad.

My Uncle Buddy, another one of my mother's brothers, lived several houses down from our trailer. He took over the farming business from my grandfather and made it more profitable than ever. He put everybody to work, even me. It didn't matter to him how old you were. If you wanted to work, he would put you on the payroll. I did everything from driving a tractor to stacking and cropping tobacco, or, "croppin' bacca" as my cousins called it. I earned my first real paycheck working for my uncle and loved every minute of it. Even though my cousins used to call me a Puerto Rican because of my fair skin, they began to accept me as part of the family. My brother, on the other hand, never could get past the bugs outside, so he usually stayed inside all day watching television.

I attended school while we were there for one year and never got into any fights. I got along with everybody. There were no gangs, drug dealers, or bullies. Just about every black kid in the school was related in one way or another. After a while, the new change became a pleasant one. Unfortunately, the only thing that didn't change was my mother's attitude toward me. She would still beat me or punish me for anything she could.

A year passed and we were still in Logan. The honeymoon phase was wearing off and I was getting bored with my surroundings. I needed some excitement, so my cousin Dean and I thought up a scheme to steal grapes from a local farmer, make moonshine, and sell it to the kids at school. Needless to say, the plan backfired because the town was so small the news of what we were doing traveled fast. My mother put a swift end to it with another one of her patented beatings.

My Uncle Tig heard about the moonshine ring and, every chance he got, he would tease me about it. He showed up one day in Logan unexpectedly. I had thought he was coming down there to tease me some more about my latest venture, but he came to tell us that he had moved to Port City, North Carolina. After being stuck in the twilight zone for a year, this news was the best I'd heard in a long time. One night, while a bunch of my cousins were sitting around cracking jokes, drinking, and wrestling with each other, he pulled me to the side and explained my mother's current situation.

"Mico, you want to know the real reason I moved down here?" he asked as he took a hit from tightly rolled joint.

"Yeah. What's up, Unk?"

"To help your mother," he said. "She has helped almost everybody in this family, and now it's time we help her."

"Help her with what?"

I really don't know why I asked such a dumb question. I knew we needed help bad. My mother was penniless and sometimes couldn't afford milk for our cereal in the mornings. We had to use powdered milk and eggs. She couldn't find steady work in Logan because of its limited industries. Working at the town store or in somebody's field was the only way people could make money there. The area was a farming industry and, because my mother's health was deteriorating, she couldn't work for long periods of time in hot weather or on her feet.

"She wants to move to Port City but can't afford to move right now," my uncle explained. "I told her I could help her out with five thousand dollars, but that's all the money I have in the world."

"How much do you need to get us out of here?"

"Your mother and I found a house she liked. We are going to need about twenty thousand to get into the house. Your Uncle Buddy said he would pitch in to help but that he would need his money back as soon as possible. I am only telling you this because you are my favorite nephew and I know you are miserable down here."

"I'm not miserable. Dontrel is the miserable one. The only time he comes out of the house is to go to school."

"If you ain't miserable, then why is your Aunt Lucy telling me that you called her at least three times asking her if you can come back to Detroit to live with her?"

"Man, she told you that?"

"Yep."

"I'm not miserable because I am in Logan. I'm miserable because of my mother."

"She still being hard on you?"

"She never lets up."

"Maybe if she was in a different situation, she'd have a better attitude."

"Maybe. But I doubt it."

"I just wanted to let you know that we are doing everything to get you guys out of here. You wanna hit this?"

He offered me the joint, and I took it. My Uncle Tig had offered me beer and liquor before, but never drugs. Just as I accepted the beer and liquor, I accepted the joint. I took a hit and almost choked to death. After a couple of more hits, I was smoking like a pro. Before the night ended, we had smoked about three more joints, and I was as high as a kite. It was a strange feeling, and I really didn't like it. All my cousins were sitting around cracking jokes on me because they knew I had virgin lungs. The feeling took me to a place where I could not contemplate what was going on around me. I liked being in control, and smoking pot affected my cognitive thinking and placed me into an increased state of paranoia. That wasn't a good feeling for me, so I never smoked again after that.

After my high wore off and everyone started leaving, I pulled my Uncle Tig to the side and told him that I had the money he needed to put my mother in the house she wanted, and that I didn't want him to tell her where the money came from.

"Where did the money come from?" asked Uncle Tig.

"It is not important where the money came from. What's important is that Momma gets the house that she wants in Port City. I will give you the money as long as you promise not to tell Momma where you got it from."

"I can't promise that I will never tell her. But I will promise that I won't tell her right now or until you become a grown man."

"Okay. I can work with that. Wait here, and I'll get the money."

I always had a suspicion that my uncle knew what I was doing when I was in Detroit because sometimes we would run into each other on the rough side of town. However, he never said anything to my mother or to me about it. Maybe it was because he had no business being in the areas where he used to see me.

I gave my uncle the money to supplement the down payment for our house in Port City without hesitation. He was my favorite uncle, and I never thought that he would cross me in any way. Besides, I knew where he lived, all I had to do was make a phone call to David, and I would have my money back with interest.

In a couple of months, my mother closed the deal on the new house and we were packing up again to move to Port City. This time, I made sure I stayed awake the entire trip. I didn't want any surprises. As we crossed the bridge into Port City, I remember seeing buildings that resembled the buildings in Detroit. They were also sidewalks, streetlights, and a familiar smell of exhaust and city sanitation. I was in heaven being back in an urban setting.

Time to Grow Up

When we arrived in Port City, we were dirt broke. I had given all of my money that I saved up from hustling with YHI to my uncle so that my mother could get the house she wanted. It didn't bother me at all because I couldn't spend all that money on myself without my mother finding out, so I didn't think twice about giving it up for our house. I would have done anything to get away from Logan.

My mother was on a fixed income and couldn't work a real job. She was receiving social security benefits and VA benefits because of my father's death. But that was just enough to pay the mortgage and pay for the bare necessities. All of our clothes were from thrift shops or five-and-dime stores. It got so bad that we had to place card board in the bottom of our sneakers because of the holes. We knew when it was time to put the cardboard in by measuring the matching holes in our socks. Another tactic we used was wearing the same pair of jeans and switching up the shirts. Sometimes, we wore the same outfit three times a week. This was the lowest period in our lives, but through it all, my mother held her end of the bargain by making sure we had something to eat, somewhere to stay, and clothes on our backs. We may have worn the same clothes every day, but they were clean. My mother always used to say that "although we might be poor, we don't have to look like it." Our clothes were always clean and pressed, including the holes.

The relationship between my mother and I got worse as I got older. I would wake up to an argument, go to school on an argument, and go to bed from an argument. It seemed whatever I did was never good enough for her. I even stopped showing her all the accolades and achievements I received in school because I felt she really didn't care about them. She had it made up in her head that I would either be in jail or dead before I turned eighteen. For a moment, I started believing her and actually started living up to her claims by acting out and living recklessly.

It was in the early eighties when I started attending high school. It seemed like all hell broke loose my first year. The girls were filling out in all the right places and the parties were happening every weekend. To me, school became a waste of time. It interfered with my booty time and party time. Although, I wasn't introduced to sex in high school, which happened earlier on in my life, I was enjoying it more. It didn't matter what nationality the girl was or even what size. If I could get it, I got it.

The only problem I had during my high school years was making the type of money that attracted the popular girls. I didn't have a car, and I worked part-time at Micky Ds after school. During my first couple of years in Port City, my mind was in a constant state of fluctuation because I was new to the area, and I didn't know what I could do to make more money. The hustle in the South was unlike the hustle in the North. Everybody knew everybody, so that made it hard to hustle or pull scams because, if you got caught, there was nowhere to run or hide. Therefore, I was forced into honest hustling. Needless to say, my high school years were pretty tame, nothing but booze, parties, and fast girls.

I barely made it to my senior year in high school and almost slipped up by letting down my guard. My mother and I were at each other throats almost every day because she hated that I was popular regardless of our economic status. With my part-time job, I could buy newer clothes and keep money in my pocket, but my brother didn't. I had friends who would pick me up so that we could hang out all night, and my brother didn't. The more I appeared to be having fun, the more my mother would try to make my life miserable. In her mind, she believed that when I was out and about, I was up to no good. Well, she was right, but I always took care of business around the house and in school.

There were many times when I felt she was being unfair and spiteful toward me, but no other incident sticks out in my head more than the time she attacked me with a broom handle and a gun for telling the truth. I don't know what was worse, her attacking me for telling the truth or her pulling a gun on me.

My cousin and I had a racket going where we would steal electronic games from stores and from the backs of semi-truck trailers, then sell them on the street. Hustles were hard to come by, so when my cousin Paul from New York introduced this idea to me, I jumped at the chance. Paul was a seasoned hustler just like me. The only difference was that he would always get caught and thrown in jail for his capers, and I never got caught. By the time I met him, he had been to jail at least three times for armed robbery, larceny, and attempted murder.

Our operation ran smooth, and we were very careful about not getting caught. We would never hit the same truck or same store twice. At times, Paul wanted to, but I refused and, if he insisted, I would tell him to go at it without me. I took pride in being a smart criminal, not a dumb one like some of the morons I used to see on television. Every caper I pulled was planned and calculated precisely. Often, Paul and I would get into arguments about the time it took for me to plan a caper. But when I used to ask him to point out a time where we got caught, he never could, so he would usually stop complaining and let me do my thing.

For a while, I felt like I was back in Detroit doing my thing. We were making some serious cash, but I knew a caper like that would have to end. The key to our success was controlling our greed; well, at least I forced us to. We could have taken truckloads of merchandise but decided against it because it would draw too much attention, so we took boxes of electronics from the center of the stack or the back of the stack. This gave the impression that it was an inside job.

We raided one truck destined for a popular local electronic store to see if the boxes contained the latest handheld electronic football games. We sifted through the boxes and, to our surprise, found the latest football games. We snatched up a couple to take home and try out. When we got back to my house, we went into my brother's room to play the games. My brother, cousin, and I stayed up all night playing them. When we finished, we stuffed them under the mattress for safekeeping.

The next day, we went to the park early in morning to play basketball before it got too hot. When we returned, my mother had a nasty look on her face. She escorted all of us to my brother's bedroom and pointed at the bed. She had laid all of the games out on the bed and asked where they came from. My cousin immediately said they were his. She told him she figured as much and to get them out of her damn house because she knew he didn't buy them. My cousin didn't argue. He scooped up the games and went outside. Then my mother asked my brother if he knew anything about the games, and he said he had no idea that they were under his bed. She then turned to me. I said I did know that they were there, that we'd been playing them the night before. After hearing this, she went ballistic. She tried to slap me, but I slipped under her swing. Then she went for the broomstick and started swinging at me. By this time, I was convinced that she had lost her mind. I grabbed the broomstick, broke it in half, and told her she wouldn't be hitting me anymore. I'd had enough.

She went into a rage and ran to get my father's old pistol. When she pointed the pistol at me, I think my brother was more scared than I was. I didn't flinch. It was my dad's gun, so I knew he was watching over me and wouldn't allow the gun to fire. I just told her that I was out of her house and that if she wanted to shoot me, she would have to shoot me in the back. I left my mother's house at age seventeen and never returned.

As I walked away from the house, I thought, *all the years of verbal and physical abuse are behind me now.* I felt liberated but not defeated. I left home with only the clothes on my back and two hundred and fifty dollars in my pocket from hustling and my last Micky D check. I had no place to go. I thought I should go live with my aunt, but I only had four months left before I graduated high school. I felt that I had come too far to fail, and I refused to let my mother or my aunt see me fail. I was going to finish high school if I had to live in the woods or in cardboard box for four months.

I remembered what my father had once told me after I got into trouble for fighting in school one time. He said that people tend to thrive off other people's failures and that there is a whole industry built on highlighting the failures of others called the media. He also said American culture will build a man up just to see how hard he falls. "Don't ever let them see you fall," he'd say. "The sweetest revenge is success."

I had nowhere to go, but I was not going to let that stop me from accomplishing my immediate goal, which was to graduate high school and move on to the next chapter in my life, whatever chapter that was. I wasn't college material, at least not yet, because I knew I lacked the self-discipline. Besides, there was no way I could pay for college, and I definitely wasn't going to ask my mother to do anything for me.

Running out of options, I caught a cab to the nearest army recruiting office, took and passed the test with high scores, and joined the army on their delayed entry program. My plan was to walk off the stage at graduation and straight into the army. I still had four months to go before graduation. I was also borderline in my math class. I had to pass that class or I wouldn't be graduating. I remember saying to myself, *here I am homeless, and all I'm concerned with is passing a damn math class.*

After leaving the recruiter's office, I found myself at one of my friend's houses, Derrick Jenkins, who we called DJ who lived in an apartment complex near my house. He and his family had come to the Port City around the same time we did. He also had a similar background. His father was killed in a gunfight in New Jersey, and his mother moved him down South to get him away from the negative influences of the big city. We connected as soon as we met each other on the basketball court. It was as if we'd known each other all of our lives. His mother was strict and abusive just like mine and never let him do anything she thought was against the "Lord's teachings." We often had to sneak out to parties together. He was the only friend I could turn to in my time of need. I managed to stay at his house for about three weeks before his mother caught on.

My next move was to go to a shelter for teens; however, their objective was to reunite teens with their families through arbitration. The reunion process usually started after four weeks. They used the four weeks as a cooling-down period, but after the cooling down period, I was gone. I didn't intend on being reunited with my mother.

After leaving the teen shelter, I called on one of my main squeezes, Angelica, who lived on the beach. Her parents were well off and had a pool house that I could have stayed in, but her house was out of my school district and was too far from the closest bus stop, so I could only spend weekends there. I also managed to spend a couple of nights at Micky Ds.

During this ordeal, I felt knocked down but not out. I refused to let my mother determine my fate, so I continued to find creative ways of staying warm at nights and making sure that I was clean and presentable for school each day. Only a handful of people knew what I was going through, and each one of them helped me through my time in need. No one else in my school had a clue, not even my teachers.

The night before graduation, I stayed at my girlfriend's house because her parents were out of town, but they let her borrow the car so that she could go to my graduation. That night we stayed up talking about the future and what we wanted out of life. I didn't have a clue what I wanted or where I was going, I just knew that I'd done so many rotten things in the past and feared that, some day, my past would catch up to me. That night, we fell asleep in each other's arms only to wake up the next morning to a show on the television called "The Lifestyles of the Rich and Famous." We lay in bed watching all the gaudy things that rich people bought with their money. I couldn't help but think what my father would say if I were to buy some of the stuff the people were buying on the show. He'd probably turn over in his grave.

They had one segment where they talked about a real-estate tycoon by the name of David Steiner. The segment not only highlighted what he bought with his riches, but it showed how he acquired all his riches and his fame. I was impressed with what I saw. Even though his story wasn't a rags to riches type story, I admired how he'd leveraged what his father started and built it into a major conglomerate of hotels and gambling casinos. That was my defining moment; I knew what I wanted to do with my life.

My graduation came and went without incident. My mother attended, and I briefly acknowledged her presence by kissing her on her forehead. I also acknowledged all the people who stuck by me through my recent ordeal. I gave my girlfriend a long kiss and proceeded to the army van, which had been sent to pick me and a couple of other graduates up. I was off to the next chapter in my life.

Life is One Big Hustle

I joined the army as a military intelligence analyst. The basic training was tough but not as tough as what I had to go through with my mother, nor was it as tough as my old neighborhood in Detroit. I had to get used to the drill sergeants getting into my face every now and then, but I just shrugged it off as part of the program. It took great restraint on my part not to swing at one of them.

I excelled in basic training, winning top honors in physical fitness and discipline along the way to include a marksmanship medal. Joining the army was the best decision I'd ever made. It was hard at times, but I couldn't see me following in my brother's footsteps by going to college; school just wasn't my thing, and there was no way I was going to give my mother another avenue of control over my life. When I left her house, I left for good. It was time for me to be my own man.

The military taught me many things: discipline, teamwork, and numerous survival skills. During basic training, I had to cope with multiple people and personalities. The screaming from the drill sergeants really didn't bother me at all because my mother's constant arguing had me prepared. Just as the drill sergeants would scream to get us up in the morning and send us to bed at night, my mother did the same thing for as long as I could remember. It was somewhat entertaining to me to say the least. It was also entertaining to watch the reaction of the other recruits. Some guys would actually break down and cry from the pressure. I actually got into fights just for laughing at the guys who I thought were weak.

Chico Jiminez was a young Mexican cat from California. He was actually a gang banger on the run from the authorities when he joined the army. He also boxed out of a local gym in Los Angeles. He had promise before he got caught up in the street life. He and I had a few choice words with one another during basic training for one reason or another but one night, during a reflection session in the barracks, the tension between us reached a boiling point.

Juan Diminguez, another Mexican from Texas, broke down crying about his experience in basic training and how hard it was for him because the drill sergeants would always pick on him for being overweight. I thought it was funny because this was the first time I'd ever seen another man cry like a baby. I couldn't help but to laugh at what I thought was a sign of weakness.

"What the fuck you laughing at, holmes?" Chico snapped.

"Diminguez, pussy ass, crying like a little bitch," I replied. "That's what I'm laughing at."

"Shut the fuck up before I give your black nigger ass something to cry about."

We were sitting on our bunks across the walkway from each other. When I heard him call me a nigger, it triggered something awful in me—something that I'd seen before and new I couldn't control. Hell, I was from Detroit and the word nigger was like the worse insult one man could bestow on another. Detroit was predominantly black, and we never used that word, not even speaking to each other. Even if a black man called you a nigger where I grew up, those were fighting words and he had to be dealt with.

Chico had to be dealt with, so I jumped off my bunk and, at the same time, he jumped off of his. The other recruits stepped out of the way because they knew that there had been tension between us since the beginning of boot camp. I guess it was because the first day I saw him, he struck me as the kind of guy

I didn't like, a bully of sorts. It was because of him that we had to do extra push-ups and run an extra mile because he wanted to give the drill sergeants some back talk. The first day we were in camp, I told him how stupid he was for trying to be so tough and to do what he was told because it would make it easier on him and everybody else. I guess I rubbed him the wrong way because, from that point forward, we became silent enemies. Well, it was finally time for us to settle our grievances and release the tension between us. We met face to face in the center of the room and, with one bump of the shoulders, it was on.

I could tell he had boxing skills by the way he moved and defended himself. However, I think he was most surprised by my skills. He was quick, but my quickness and power overwhelmed him. Not only was he shocked by my skills, but I also shocked all the recruits as well as Drill Sergeant Brown who had been standing behind me. After the smoke cleared, Chico was left with a broken nose, cracked jaw, and sore ribs, and I was left with permanent kitchen detail.

Drill Sergeant Brown was so impressed by the way I'd handled myself that he recommended me for the army boxing program. I didn't realize it at first, but Sergeant Brown's recommendation carried some weight; he'd been an army boxing champion who went on to win a bronze medal in the Olympics. He became a huge inspiration to me and I didn't want to let him down, so I made sure that I concentrated on becoming the best recruit ever. I trained hard and followed all the rules. Even though I was stuck on kitchen detail for the remainder of my time in boot camp, I kept a level head and exceeded all the challenges that were given to me. Chico was also placed on kitchen detail and, needless to say, there was never tension between us again. In fact, we became the best of friends.

After boot camp, Chico and I went to separate army training schools. He signed up for special forces and I went on to military intelligence training. After military school, I started boxing for the army and was on my way to the Olympic trials when an overzealous commander decided boxing did not take precedence over training for a military mission. He ordered me to join a field-training exercise with the rest of my company. Of course, I had no choice but to follow orders. Unfortunately, the field-training exercise ended my boxing career.

During the exercise, I was riding in an all-terrain vehicle when it flipped from a sudden turn. I was thrown from the vehicle and landed on my head. Luckily, I was wearing my Kevlar helmet, so I didn't sustain too much damage, but I felt an unbearable sharp pain in my lower back, so much so that I couldn't walk for days. It turned out that I didn't need surgery but would be left with a permanent back injury that couldn't be fixed. I refused to let the injury prevent me from accomplishing my dreams of being an Olympic champion and, after a great deal of rehabilitation, I resumed my training in the ring. I could tell that I wasn't the same boxer, but I didn't want the coach or my teammates to know that I wasn't one hundred percent. I fought back the pain and trained as hard as I could. My goal was to go on to the national championships and eventually the Olympic trials.

We had a tune-up match with the Korean national team before the national championships. This was an opportunity for me to make a comeback and to show my team that I was still their top prospect for winning a spot at the Olympics. The night of the fight, my back felt good. During warm-ups, I could move side to side like I used to with ease and throw my signature punch—the left jab followed by a left hook. I was ready.

When the bell rang, I went to work and had the crowd on their feet for two straight rounds. I was pounding my opponent and giving him the boxing lesson of his life. By the third and final round, I felt good. Everyone was amazed that my opponent was still standing after taking so much punishment. The bell rang for the third round, and the first punch I threw was my signature punch, but after the left hook landed, I felt a sharp pain in my lower back. It felt like I was paralyzed. I couldn't pull my punch back fast enough before my opponent landed a straight right hand. I fell back against the ropes and assumed a fetal position because I couldn't move. I finally managed to land a right cross, but that was all I had left. He hit me to the body, and I fell to my knees. I couldn't continue. This was the first loss of my amateur career. The loss was hard for me to bear. I was devastated at the thought of not being able to box again and, worse, not being able to defend myself on the street.

After a year passed, the devastation of losing a fight finally wore off but returned briefly as I watched two of my teammates go on to win medals at the Olympics. I was happy for them but saddened that I couldn't be with them on the winning podium. I always felt that my mother was cursing me because she never wanted me to box in the first place. My goal was to prove her wrong, but it was out of my control. To get my mind off boxing, I started concentrating on my job. I wanted to learn everything I could about military intelligence from the technology to the covert methods that were used to acquire confidential information. Twice, I was deployed overseas to gather information on enemy activity from North Korea and East Germany. That was exciting work for me because I was able to be somebody I wasn't with the support of a whole country behind me.

After the missions were completed, I was sent to a naval base in San Diego. I was attached to an adjutant general unit because the military felt I needed to be deprogrammed and they didn't want me to take on a job that would be too stressful. When I arrived at the unit, I was assigned to the military identification card issuance office, basically making identification cards for military personnel and their dependants. It was a cool and non-stressful assignment and just what I needed after being cooped up in an underground vault overseas for two years. It wasn't as exciting as my previous job, but I could deal with it because I only had a year and half left in the military with no intentions on reenlisting.

My new job quickly became very mundane and boring. I remember thinking to myself that there had to be a way for me to make the job more exciting and, to my surprise, I did. It turned out that my new roommate, Zee Haskins, worked in the same department but in the area where the identification cards were actually manufactured. I only worked on the processing desk, where the applications for the new cards were initially processed. The applicants would give me the applications to review before advancing to the next station. Zee worked in the area where all the fun took place. I used to hear them laughing and carrying on in the back like they were having a party every day. Come to find out they had a reason to celebrate because, apparently, they were making a lot of money on the side. Not only were they manufacturing regular identification cards, they were also mass-producing fake military identification cards for prepaid customers. Zee didn't want to tell me at first because he didn't know if I was working undercover, but he eventually did after finding out that I was cool.

"Yo man, what the hell be going on in the back at work?" I asked Zee as we returned to our room in the barracks after a long day at work.

"What do you mean, potna?" Zee replied.

"It seems like you guys are always having a fucking party back there."

"We are. You just got to make the best of this hell hole."

Zee was from North Carolina, but you would never know it because he didn't have a Southern drawl. His mode was always neutral and laid back, never stressed out about anything. We connected the first time we met. He had been in San Diego for about three months before I got there and had checked the place out thoroughly. He knew every club, gambling joint, hustler hangout, weed spot, and where all the top-notched women hung out. It was like I'd hit the jackpot by having him as my roommate. We had a lot in common and often talked about our lives until the break of dawn.

"Yeah. I'm trying to figure out how the hell I can make the best out of my boring-ass job," I said as I threw my boots in the corner of the room.

"Bitch job, huh man?"

"Sho right. I feel like a little bitch taking applications. Smiling all the time and saying 'hi, can I help you?' and 'next in line please,'" I said as I mimicked a Micky D employee.

We both laughed.

"Yeah, that is some lame-ass shit." Zee sparked a joint and opened a window. He then threw me a towel. "Dog, stuff that under the door."

"Hey man, how can I get back there with you?"

"I don't know, bro. It's kinda tight back there now. I can probably talk to the sarge and see if I can get you a spot. We're actually trying to get rid of this one dude back there anyway. He's fucking up the program."

"What, he holding up production?"

"You can say that." He offered me the joint.

"I can't fuck with that homey."

"What's up, man? You CID?"

"Naw man. I just can't fuck with it because it fucks with my head."

"Hell, that's what it's suppose to do. You think I smoke because I like the smell?"

Although, I was in military intelligence, I wasn't part of the Central Intelligence Division— CID That was a separate division. I was sworn to secrecy, so I couldn't tell Zee what unit I was attached too. Besides, I didn't want him to think I was there to spy on him and his crew. I knew by me not accepting the joint I'd draw unwarranted suspicion, so I had to counter quickly.

"I can't smoke that shit, but if you got some crank or some of that white girl, we can talk."

"Oh hell, you roll like that. Well, let me finish this, and I'll see what I can drum up for you."

Cocaine became my drug of choice ever since I'd been introduced to it during my tour overseas. I used to make cocaine drops when I was in YHI but never tried it. After trying it for the first time in Korea, I liked it because it didn't make me zone out. It actually made me more alert and gave me more energy. After one of my partners, Smitty, introduced me to it while hanging out with some Korean women, I was hooked. I wasn't hooked in a sense that I became a junky, but hooked in the sense that it was my drug of choice.

"So you gonna hook me up?"

"You know I got the hook up. Anything you need, I got it."

"No, I don't mean the powder. I'm talking about the spot in the back."

"Spot in the back? Oh yeah, I got that covered too. Don't worry about that. I'll get you back there, but you gotta understand something."

"What's that?"

"We put in work back there."

"I'm not afraid of hard work," I replied.

"Naw, I mean we put in extra work. The kind that can get you locked up."

"How so?"

That's when Zee told me all about the operation and how they were making extra money by changing the birth dates on the identification cards for military personnel and dependants who were underage. They had a full-fledged fake ID operation going on in addition to producing the regular identification cards. They also had a mail-order operation for people who responded to small ads placed in a couple of magazines. People were receiving authentic United States military ID cards in the mail. The word was out in the underground and all a person had to do was pay fifty dollars to make it happen. For mail order, it was one hundred and fifty dollars. I wasn't aware of how lucrative it was until I finally got to the back. The rest of the team accepted me with open arms because they trusted Zee. Besides, he was running the show. Of course, that was the case before I joined. After participating in the operation for a little while, I came up with innovative ways to improve the manufacturing and distribution of the fake ID cards. We were making thousands of extra dollars each week.

After running a smooth operation for several months, we decided to move out of the barracks and into a two-bedroom apartment not far from the base. We made our deposit on the place but couldn't move in for a couple of weeks because we had to wait for the old tenants to move out. That meant we had to stay in the barracks a little while longer. I hated living in the barracks because it was too cramped and everybody knew everybody's business. I was anxious to get out of there. I didn't want to make any new friends. All I wanted was to concentrate on our operation and make sure that we didn't get caught. I was suspicious of any new faces and anyone who appeared to want to infiltrate our space. It was hard because everybody liked Zee. He was an extrovert and I was an introvert. Zee managed to bring someone new to the room almost every day. If it wasn't a weed-smoking buddy, it was a fine-ass female friend. Although, I liked and trusted Zee, I knew with this type of behavior we couldn't do too many capers together.

The day came for us to move out of the barracks. As we were packing our things, I heard a knock on our room door. I figured it was probably one of Zee's buddies coming by to wish us luck, but when I opened the door, I came face to face with First Sergeant McDuff and a lieutenant whom I've never seen before. I immediately snapped to attention as we were trained to do in the presence of an officer.

"At ease soldier," responded Sergeant McDuff.

"Specialist Brunson and Specialist Haskins?" asked the lieutenant.

"Yes sir," Zee and I responded simultaneously.

"Please come with me."

Without question, we grabbed our headgear and followed the lieutenant out of the barracks with our first sergeant trailing behind us. We started in the direction of the headquarters building, and I immediately knew what the visit was all about, but instead of panicking, I started thinking of a plan of action. Zee and I glanced at each other several times. And with the last glance, I gave him a nod to indicate that I would take care of it. We never rehearsed what we would say if we got caught, so I was depending on Zee's wit to help us through. I knew what my plan was, but Zee didn't have a clue. I knew they would interrogate us separately, but I just hoped they would keep us together long enough for Zee to pick up on my strategy. They didn't. In fact, as soon as we entered the building, we were shuffled to separate interrogation rooms.

As I entered the room, I noticed two men sitting at a conference table dressed in Class-A uniforms. I immediately identified their rank. One was a captain and the other was a warrant officer II.

"Have a seat, soldier," the captain ordered.

"Yes sir," I replied.

"Are you Specialist Mico Brunson?"

"Yes sir."

"This session will be recorded, Specialist Brunson. I am Captain Baker and this is Warrant Officer Jones. We are from the Central Intelligence Division. Do you know why you are here?"

"No, sir, I don't."

"You are here, Specialist, because we have reason to believe you are engaged in the illegal activity of manufacturing fake military identification cards."

"Oh, that," I responded with a sense of relief.

It was time for me to put my plan in action. I knew they had to know what my military occupational skill was and probably knew what I did for my last assignment, so I had to leverage my position.

"Yes, that," Warrant Officer Jones replied. "Are you not denying your involvement?"

"No, sir, I'm not. I was on a mission."

"A mission?" asked Captain Baker. "What mission might this be and who commissioned it?"

"I was undercover. It was my intention to brief the company commander, but I had to make sure that I knew the details of the operation and who all the players were."

"Who commissioned this mission soldier?" asked Captain Baker.

"No one, sir."

"No one, soldier?"

"No sir. I took the initiative on my own after learning of the potential illegal activity that was going on in my unit."

"You took the initiative without informing your superiors?" chimed Warrant Officer Jones.

"Yes sir. As I stated before, I had to."

"You had to know the details of the operation," interrupted Warrant Officer Jones.

"And the players, sir," I respond with a little irritation in my voice.

"Okay, soldier, you now have the opportunity to share the details of your mission with us."

Gathering my thoughts, I pulled out a little writing pad that I used to jot down the details of the mission. I actually anticipated getting caught, so I had prepared the notes a week before. My notes were in chronological order as if I were capturing the details as they happened. I even crumpled up some of the pages and used different color pens to make it appear more authentic. After describing the mission in detail as I rehearsed it in my mind on the way to headquarters, the CID agents asked me to step out of the room while they discussed the findings with my superior officers. I didn't know what to expect as I sat in the waiting area. In my details, I had identified Zee as my accomplice in the undercover mission and our squad leader as the ringleader of the illegal activity. I didn't know what Zee had told the agents who interrogated him. I just hoped that he'd remained neutral.

That day was the longest day in my military career. I kept thinking that, after all the illegal activity I'd had been involved in as a kid, I had to get caught on a penny hustle as an adult, a hustle that could have caused me problems for the rest of my life. I could have been sent to Leavenworth and receive a dishonorable discharge from the army. We made good money with this hustle, but it wasn't worth the consequences.

Zee and I didn't get to see each other until later that night. I got back to the barracks before he did and had to deal with the stares and the questions from everybody in the barracks. I simply brushed them off and anxiously awaited Zee's arrival. When Zee finally got back to the barracks, we embraced each other and started in on the tales of our experience with the CID agents. Just as I expected, Zee remained neutral throughout the questioning. He just told them that he wasn't aware of what was going on behind the scenes and that his involvement was simply delivering the fake IDs to the customers in the waiting room. I told him how I executed my plan and we spent the rest of the night preparing for follow-up questioning just in case.

The next day, we were summoned to the headquarters again where we received a written reprimand, a field grade Article 15 and orders confining us to our barracks for thirty days for our involvement in the illegal ID operation without informing our superiors. Apparently, my plan had worked. This was literally a slap on the wrist compared to what could have happened. Our ordeal was finally over, and we partied for the next thirty days.

As soon as the thirty days passed, we moved into our apartment together. The living arrangements were perfect. We were ideal roommates because we liked all of the same things— liquor, beautiful women, and getting high. We understood and respected each other's space, women, and drugs. I could leave a couple of lines on the coffee table while I went out to run errands and, when I returned, the lines would still be there. I didn't worry about Zee messing with my stuff, and he didn't worry about me messing with his. We had a great time together as roommates and as fellow soldiers. Often, we would have competitions to see who could shine their shoes the best or shine their brass for their Class As the best. We were outstanding soldiers who often were recognized by our units for outstanding work.

Booze, Drugs, and Love

After the dust settled with the ID scam, we received reassignment orders to Fort Carson, Colorado, located in Colorado Springs, where we worked in different units. Zee went to a contractual supply unit, and I went to work for the adjutant general, attached to a military intelligence unit where I would screen soldiers' backgrounds before they were placed on covert missions. It was a challenging position for me because sometimes I would come face to face with disgruntled commanders or first sergeants who thought that I should ignore their selected soldiers' negative backgrounds and send them on their assigned missions. It made them even angrier when they saw that they did not intimidate me and would often kick them out of my office and refer them to the post commander for further review. I had power in my position and our post commander backed up that power.

Zee and I became highly dedicated and decorated soldiers. That, of course, was only while we were on the clock. In our own time, we were a couple of partying womanizing fools who often got caught up in unusual situations. Like the time we were invited by one of Zee's partners to go to a Run DMC concert in Denver. Eddie Molson was from Denver and was assigned to Zee's unit. He became a good friend who often provided the drugs for all the parties. At the time, we didn't know Molson used to be a well-known drug dealer and gang member in Denver before running off to the military. As the story goes, the Crips migrated to Denver from California to set up a major distribution point for drugs and guns. Molson was recruited through his older brother to join the operation. The operation got so big that the FBI and DEA were involved with tracking down some of the key members of the gang and bringing them to justice. His brother was one of the key members.

The authorities had surveillance video of some illegal activity, and Molson was one of the culprits on the video, but before he could be identified, he joined the military and spent two years in Germany and one year in Korea before being shipped to Fort Carson. He still had ties to the gang but wasn't actively involved in illegal gang activity anymore. At least, that was what he told us.

The night of the concert, Molson had promised us a night of drugs, women, and wild fun and, to my amazement, he delivered. We filled four carloads of soldiers and went to Denver, about seventy miles north of Colorado Springs. When we arrived at Molson's house, which he inherited from his parents, we were shocked and pleased to see all the drugs, booze, and, yes, women. The women were already there and waiting to party. I was on cloud nine because I had access to all the cocaine and booze I wanted, free of charge.

Just as I was finishing my fifth line, I caught an image of beauty out the corner of my eye. This girl was gorgeous as hell, with all the right curves in all the right places. She stood about five-feet six-inches tall, had short wavy hair, hazel eyes, and smooth coconut-tinted skin.

"You gonna save some for me?" she whispered.

"How could I say no?" I asked as I brushed the residue off my nose.

I couldn't help but to notice the Jamaican accent. I offered her my homemade straw, which was a tightly rolled dollar bill, but she declined and pulled out a gold container from her purse.

"Excuse me. I didn't realize you were a pro," I said.

"No. Not at all," she replied. "Just prepared."

"I like that," I responded as I stepped aside to let her do her thing. "You from the Islands?"

She took a good toke in both nostrils and leaned back to catch the flow and the full effect of the hit.

"Yes, ahhh," she said as she felt the cocaine tickling her nostrils. "I am from Jamaica."

"Then I guess it's true what they say about Jamaica."

"What's that?"

"That Jamaica produces the most beautiful women in the world."

"Ah, that's sweet, corny, but sweet."

Just as I was about to build off that corny line, Molson summoned everyone to take his or her last drink or hit so we could make it to the concert on time. Rather than making more conversation with the vision of beauty I just met, I decided getting my last toke in was more important and so did she. We took our last hit and left for the concert in separate cars. While at the concert, I could not take my eyes off her. It was as if I were in a trance. I couldn't understand what she had that made me want her so bad. I'd been with plenty of beautiful women, but it was something about this one that had me captivated.

After the concert, Molson wanted to go to an after party in his old neighborhood. I really didn't want to go because I wanted to get back to the house so that I could talk more to the Jamaican beauty. But Molson took a vote and we wound up going to the party.

I became uneasy as we pulled into the neighborhood where the party was taking place. It was a house party and I hated house parties. Especially, house parties that were thrown by people I didn't know. I was an outsider and most house parties were thrown for people in the neighborhood, not outsiders. Zee and I both felt the same about it and didn't want to go in. The house was packed and the overflow was outside on the front lawn and in the backyard. It appeared that everyone was having a good time and Molson, with the help of the girls, convinced us to join the party.

"Man, these are my peeps," said Molson. "Nothing is going to pop off."

"How long are we gonna be here, potna?" asked Zee.

"Ten minutes tops."

As we approached the party, we caught the stares and glares of some of the guys hanging out on the porch. Molson apparently knew them because he gave them daps as we went in. We had some fine-ass women on our arms, and I just knew all it would take was some jealous punk to start some trouble. Just as I suspected, as soon as we walked in the door, it started. Someone grabbed the ass of the girl Molson was with and she went off. Molson had some choice words with the guy, but before I could intervene, the issue was squashed.

It was so crowded in there that my paranoia would not allow me to stay, so I decided to go back on the porch. I took the hand of my Jamaican queen and led her back onto the porch. Molson and Zee proceeded to the back of the house with their women in tow.

"Are you scared?" she asked.

"No. This just isn't my type of scene. I hate crowds. I felt uneasy even at the concert."

"Paranoid, huh?"

"Yes, very. That's what keeps me alive."

"Paranoia?"

"I call it controlled paranoia."

She laughed and gave me a tight hug. I could feel her firm breasts pressed up against my chest. I returned the gesture just to get an opportunity to smell her sweet fragrance and touch her soft silky skin. As we pulled away, our lips connected and, like magic, we engaged in a long passionate kiss. I was hooked.

"Excuse me," I teased. "But I don't know you like that."

"Oh, I am sorry," she said and stepped back and extended her hand. "It's a pleasure to meet you. My name is Jasmine. And what is your name?"

"Hi, my name is Mico." I took her hand a pressed it against my lips. "Now that we got that out of the way." I grabbed her by her waist and pull her up against me once again. We engaged in a longer kiss. I was so entranced by her presence that I didn't realize Molson and Zee had abruptly left the party.

"Hey, aren't those your partners?" Jasmine asks as she pointed at Molson and Zee walking down the middle of the street.

"Yeah, I guess it's time to leave."

I grabbed her hand and started walking down the street but, unbeknownst to me, we were being followed by what seemed to be every guy from the party. I heard someone call out, "Hey, that's one of them right there."

Instead of ignoring them, I decided to stop to see what all the ruckus was about.

"What's the problem?" I asked.

"You the problem, punk!" someone yelled out.

At that point, I felt reasoning with a crowd of angry knuckleheads wasn't a wise thing to do, so the liquor and cocaine told me to punch the guy closest to me in the face.

"Hey, that's my cousin," yelled someone from the mob.

"I don't give a fuck," I responded as I began swinging.

My temper, liquor, and machismo took over, and I found myself in the middle of the street fighting the entire crowd. I thought I was doing pretty good and was holding my own until somebody slipped behind me and hit me on the back of the head with something.

I blanked out. The next thing I remember was Jasmine standing over me, helping me to my feet.

"What happened?" I asked, still weary from the blow.

"It don't matter," Jasmine replied. "You're okay now. Let's go."

I looked around and caught a glimpse of the crowd. They were now at a distance because Molson was standing behind us with his gun drawn. Zee apparently tried to come to my aid but was also jumped by the crowd. He suffered a nasty blow to the eye.

We made it back to our cars without further incident and drove back to Molson's place. As soon as we entered the house, Jasmine started nursing the knot on the back of my head, and the girl who was with Zee nursed his eye.

"You are a fool," said Jasmine. "What possessed you to try to fight all those thugs?"

"My father told me never to run from a fight because, if I got caught, I would be too tired to defend myself."

"Yeah, but to try to fight fifty thugs is suicide."

"I'd rather die a warrior than a coward."

"You crazy."

"Yeah, about you."

We kissed again and spent the rest of the night drinking, getting high, and getting to know each other.

After that night, Jasmine and I became inseparable. When she wasn't in school or studying for an exam, she was with me. When I wasn't working or pulling duty, I was with her. We talked about marriage on several occasions but felt it would be best after she graduated from the University of Denver and started her career. I didn't really want to get married while I was in the military because, at any time, I could have been reassigned to somewhere where we couldn't be together.

My womanizing days were over, at least, that's what I wanted to think. But as fate would have it, Jasmine's mother fell ill in New York and she had to quit school to take care of her. I was devastated of the thought of losing the woman I loved, the woman who taught me how to love and how to make love. She was very passionate in life and in bed. She introduced me to so many different things that, even though I was far from being a virgin when I met her, I always felt she was the one who took my virginity. Now, after six months of intense passion and love, we had to part.

Before she left for New York, I gave her a solid gold necklace with a St. Mary's medallion that had my initials and the inscription "My world, my life" on the back. After she left, we tried the long distance love affair thing. I paid for her to come visit me in Colorado a couple of times, and I even met up with her in D.C. on two occasions but, eventually, our lives took us in separate directions and we stopped calling and writing each other. I went back to my old ways.

Vengeance is Mine

The bond between Zee and I grew even closer after the incident in Denver. It was like we became blood brothers. After my relationship with Jasmine dissolved, we started taking trips to different places—Las Vegas, New Mexico, and Mexico—and partying hard at every stop. Unfortunately, all the partying and all the trips couldn't erase what happened in Denver. The Denver incident was far behind us, but I couldn't help thinking of how I got knocked out for the first time in my life. It bothered me so bad that I had to get my revenge and, eventually, so did Zee. We decided to wait until we both had about one month left in the military before we made our move.

We approached Molson for some information.

"You wanna do what?" asked Molson.

"They gotta be dealt with," I responded.

"Man, that's water under the bridge."

"That's what I want them to think. Just point the fools out to us. That's all you have to do."

"Molson, my eye still hurts from that shit," snapped Zee as he rubbed his eye.

"Man, I know how you feel, but you niggas got off easy. Do you realize who those fools were?"

"I don't give a fuck who they are," I said, getting angrier from Molson's obvious brush off. "Those motherfuckers knocked me out."

"Those motherfuckers could have killed you. They were Crips."

"Crips?" asked Zee.

"Yeah, Crips. And the only reason they didn't kill you is because you were with me."

"Because we was with you?" I snapped. "Nigga, we got jumped because we was with you. What the fuck you talkin' 'bout?"

Molson went on to tell us how this gang member named Dane always resented the fact that he ran to the military to get away from some trouble that he helped the Crips start. Molson wanted to end the friction, but Dane didn't want to because he thought Molson was shady and thought he had turned state's evidence against some of the members.

None of that really mattered to me. I just wanted to settle a score. When it came to fighting, my Uncle Tig would always say, "A man may beat me today in a fight, but he would definitely lose tomorrow." I had to settle the score.

"Okay, okay," said Molson. "If you niggas want to take it to the next level, then I'll point the fools out to you. The Teen Celebration is happening in Denver this weekend, so we can do it then. I know they'll be there. They always are. Besides, I hate that nigga Dane anyway. So you niggas do what you have to do."

"Cool," I replied. "Then it's on."

"One warning, though, Dane stays strapped, so you better be ready to fire on that fool."

"Nigga, I'm from Detroit, me firing on a fool has never been a problem. You just point him out and I'll do the rest."

Before the weekend came, Zee and I went to a local pawnshop to purchase a couple of pistols. At no time did we ever give it a second thought nor did our consciences kick in.

We followed Molson to Denver in a different car because we didn't know if he would flake out and do something stupid like leave us stranded. Besides, I had to map out a route for the getaway, and I didn't want to depend on someone else driving.

The Teen Celebration was an annual event in Denver, but it was on the verge of being cancelled because of all the gang problems that started over the past couple of years. It was held downtown on the main street. I was familiar with downtown enough to know how to get out of there quickly.

When we arrived, there were police and barricades everywhere and some serious tension was already in the air. Apparently, something must have popped off before we got there because police were walking around in riot gear, but there were still people walking around partying and having fun. We finished mapping out our escape route and strategically parked our cars for an easy getaway.

Molson knew we were strapped and ready to deal with Dane and his crew. He seemed kind of nervous, so I was starting to lose my confidence in him. I wasn't sure if he was going to turn on us because of his loyalty to his gang, so I watched his every move. We followed him up and down the street, searching for our target. An hour had passed and still no Dane. Fights were starting to break out all around us and the police were getting restless. Then, all of a sudden, a big ruckus occurred one block in front of us and everybody seemed to go wild. The scene got real crazy, and we didn't want any part of it.

As soon as we turned to get out of there, the police started firing tear gas from the ground and from the police helicopter that was hovering above. We started running to our cars and, as fate would have it, we turned the corner and ran smack into Dane and two other gang members. The scene was chaotic by now, and all I could remember was us facing off with Dane once again for a brief moment.

"That's him?" I asked Molson in a loud tone.

"Yeah," Molson answered. "That's him."

"So what, punk?" yelped Dane as he and his crew walked toward us.

Without a word and without any warning, I pulled out my gun and started firing. All three gang members stopped in their tracks and all I heard was "oh shit, I'm hit." Zee never had a chance to pull his gun. We turned and made a mad dash to our cars and, keeping with Detroit's tradition, I didn't stay to see them fall.

As we drove calmly through the streets, following our escape route to the highway, I instructed Zee to dismantle the gun and through the pieces out of the window every five miles. I had already scratched off the serial numbers before we went to Denver, so all that was left to do was get rid of the evidence. Zee followed my instructions without question.

"Man I didn't know you was that crazy," Zee said as he threw pieces of the gun out of the window.

"I'm not crazy. I'm thorough."

We made it back to our apartment without incident. I wasn't concerned about being caught at all because the conditions were perfect. The scene was chaotic, noisy, and dark, a perfect scene for a perfect hit. I spent the rest of the night convincing Molson and Zee that we didn't have anything to worry about. Molson was more concerned about the possibility that Dane or one of the gang members would still be alive. If so, they would definitely come after him. Of course, I wasn't concerned about that because, in a couple of days, I would be out of the army and out of Colorado and so would Zee. Molson would have to deal with any repercussions on his own. Besides, it was because of him that I was knocked out and on the verge of being killed and Zee suffered a permanent eye injury.

A New Page to Turn

The day came when I had to make a decision to either reenlist or get out of the army. I chose to get out of the army because I felt that I had accomplished all that I wanted to accomplish. I had traveled to places where most people only dream of and acquired the discipline, experience, and work ethic that I needed to be successful in life. I decided to get out and face the world at another level, but I had nowhere to go.

There was no way I was going back to live at my mother's house, even though we had talked several times while I was in the army and somewhat reconciled our differences. I wasn't convinced that things would be different if I moved back. Besides, through the abuse, she had at least taught me to be independent and self-sufficient, and I still had something to prove.

With nowhere to go, I contacted my brother who had moved to Charlotte, North Carolina, after graduating from North Carolina State University with a business degree. He had his own life, but I knew our bond was strong enough that he would never turn me away. As suspected, he welcomed me with open arms. I packed my things and moved to Charlotte. I offered Zee an opportunity to come along, because I knew my brother wouldn't mind, but he declined and, to my surprise, he reenlisted. Like me, he really didn't have any home to go back to and, rather than take a gamble on civilian life, he chose to stay in the army and was shipped to Germany.

When I arrived at my brother's place, we spent the next couple of weeks catching up and getting reacquainted with each other. He was not concerned with all the negative events in my past, so we never discussed them, just the positive stuff. I was surprised at how college made him loosen up a little. He actually became a party-hopping womanizing fool, just like his little brother. It was a great time but a time that I knew couldn't last forever. I was too independent, and I didn't want to depend on anyone, even if it was my own brother. I knew he loved me enough to let me live with him indefinitely, but I wanted something more, something more than he or Charlotte, North Carolina, could offer. I wanted to be a successful businessman like David Steiner, my idol. I needed to be in an environment that would give me the right opportunity. Charlotte was not the right environment to make this happen because it wasn't fast paced enough for me, and it still had that Southern stigma when it came to providing opportunities for the black man. I thought about going back to Detroit to live with my aunt, but that thought quickly faded when I thought of all the bad memories of my father's murder, the economic struggles, and all the skeletons I had left behind. I needed a fresh start, a fresh city.

My unemployment insurance was running out, and I had to make a move soon. As luck would have it, DJ, my childhood friend from Port City, got my contact information from my mother. Apparently, he was looking for a fresh start also. He came to Charlotte to hang out with my brother and me for a couple of weeks before moving to Washington, D.C.

"Yo, man, I'm telling you that this could be the move," exclaimed DJ.

"Shit sounds too much like a real job," I replied.

"In the beginning, yes, but we could get in there and make a killing."

"So this guy you know, will he hire me without an investment background?"

"Hell yeah, they're looking for as many sharp brothers as they can get, and it's legit."

"Legit? Man, I do better at crime than I do at legit," I laughed as I snorted another line.

"It's time to make a change, my brother. Let's take it to the next level. Those white boys run game and bullshit their way in the door all the time. Why can't we do the same thing?"

"You know I'm willing to try anything at least once. Hell, I hear the ratio of women to men in D.C. is about seven to one. Now that's my kind of odds."

"We need to make the money first, my brother, and the women will follow."

"You got that right. I'm game. It's nothing but another fucking hustle anyway, just on a different block."

DJ wanted me to go with him to D.C. and work for a private investment firm that a friend of his turned him on to while he was in the Air Force. I was ready for a change so, quite naturally, I accepted the challenge. After we got our next unemployment check, we left for D.C. immediately. We decided to leave on a Monday morning because we wanted to give ourselves at least one full week so that we could set up an interview with the investment company and find an apartment.

Upon arriving, we didn't know anyone nor did we know where we were going to live. DJ contacted the guy from the investment company to set up a date and time for an interview, but we still had to find a place to stay. Luckily, DJ used to date a girl from D.C. He knew how to get around and he knew about some of the worst and best places to live. We grabbed a newspaper and started searching. Our money wasn't long so we had to find a place where we could afford to pay for the first month's rent and have enough left over for gas and food. We found a spot right outside of D.C. just across the Maryland border.

The advertisement said that it was only two hundred and seventy five dollars per month for a furnished two-bedroom apartment. I guess we should have known that there was a catch.

When we arrived during the day, it was hot. The streets were clear and the area looked well-maintained. The furniture in the apartment turned out to be a burlap covered couch, loveseat, a patched-up coffee table, a four-piece yard sale dinette set, and two cot-like beds. The window air conditioner worked well because the temperature in the apartment was very cool. We paid our deposit plus one month's rent, dropped off our bags, and headed for downtown D.C.

We spent some time bar hopping during happy hour. The scene was too buppyish for me but DJ liked it because it fit his style. We really didn't make any connections, just engaged in a lot of small talk with a couple locals.

On our way back to the apartment, DJ wanted to stop by a strip club, but I discouraged him by reminding him we had to conserve money because we weren't going to see an unemployment check for another two weeks. He snapped out of his excitement and we made our way back to the apartment.

As we drove up to the neighborhood, I noticed the scene had drastically changed. It was now nighttime, and there were hoards of young black men hovering and mingling in the area. Some approached the car as we drove up to our apartment, offering to sell us drugs. DJ and I were caught off guard and had to conceal our shock. I couldn't help but to think that they were going to see our North Carolina tags and rob us. But I kept my cool and parked the car near our new apartment. The scene was crazy and seemed like something out of a movie. I wanted to park my car in front of our building but couldn't because the parking lot was full. I had to park it on the side of the building out of view of the apartment. When I stepped out of the car, I braced myself for what I thought would be the inevitable—us getting jumped. But that didn't happen. The guys stopped following the car when they saw us parking and walked away.

We walked passed a couple of guys smoking a joint and entered the apartment building like we had always lived there. Once inside, we ran into two groups of guys shooting crap in the hallway. One group was directly in front of the door leading to our apartment and, instead of me slipping past the group of thugs to go into my apartment, I asked if I could join the game.

"What they hittin' fo' yo?" I asked.

"Buy in at five, son," murmured someone from the group. "You in?"

"True dat," I responded. "I'm in."

DJ shook his head and went into the apartment under the watchful eye of a couple guys who were bent down enjoying the game. The game was going fast, and I was next up on the dice. I made a couple of good licks but crapped out on my fifth throw. I stayed in the game for a long while and, when it was all said and done, I was up one hundred and fifty dollars. The guys couldn't tell if I was winning or not because I was secretly slipping money in my pocket rather than leaving it on floor. After stuffing the money, I stayed in the game with about fifty dollars showing. I played on fifty dollars for about two hours before losing and giving them the impression I was broke.

"I'm out dog," I squelched. "You niggas broke me."

"All right, playa," said one of the guys. "Go get some more money, nigga, and come see us tomorrow."

I gave some of the players a few daps and went into the apartment. They never asked who I was nor did I care who they were. It was all about the money.

The next day, I woke up ready to face our new life in D.C. I peered out of the window just to see if there were any remnants from the previous night. There wasn't a soul in sight. It was like the night before never happened, but I was reassured it did happen when I reached into my pocket and pulled out the hundred dollars I had won.

"Man, you're a nut case," DJ said as he walked into the kitchen rubbing the sleep out of his eyes.

"How so, dog?"

"Those fools could have jacked you last night."

"Jack who?" I raised my voice as I slammed the hundred dollars I won on the kitchen table. "I jacked them fools!"

"Oh shit! How much you hit'em for?"

"A bone."

"Then I guess that means the club is on you tonight."

"Yep, yep. I think I'm going to love D.C."

We both laughed as we contemplated what we were going to eat for breakfast. With nothing in the cupboard, we geared up and were off to find the closest IHOP. But, to my dismay, my car was gone. At first, I wanted to believe that I parked in a no-parking zone and it was towed but, unfortunately, that wasn't the case.

"What the fuck?" I screamed as I grabbed my head and sat on the curb where my car had been. "The motherfuckers stole my car! I can't believe this shit."

"Shit!" said DJ. "What the hell are we gonna do now?"

Hearing all the moans, a young brother emerged from what appeared to be his work van and approached us.

"Yo, dog," said the young brother. "They got you, huh man?"

"Yeah, the bastards got me," I snapped.

"What kind of car was it?"

"A black Mustang. Did you see it?"

"Yeah, I saw it last night when I came in about eleven thirty. It had North Carolina tags."

"Yep. You see anybody around it?"

"Naw, man, these little niggas around here are slick. They ain't gonna do nothin' but ride up and down the streets until the gas run out of it. Was it manual or automatic?"

"Manual. Hey, you got a phone in your crib? I need to call the cops."

"Yeah, hold on a minute while I git some shit out of my van."

"All right man, thanks."

DJ and I followed him back to his van.

"You need some help?" asked DJ.

"Yeah, grab that table saw and pick axe."

"Man, you look a little familiar," I said as I grabbed the axe from the van. "Where you from?"

"Dallas, Texas, potna."

"Dallas? How the hell you get to D.C.?"

"It's a long story but the short version is my bitch ass ex-wife. I met her while I was stationed in Fort Lee, Virginia."

"So you were in the army."

"Yep, I got out about a year and a half ago and followed her ass back here. She got back with her peeps and went buck wild. She got strung out and I left her ass."

"Were you ever at Fort Carson?"

"Yeah, that was my last station."

"Oh shit, mine too. That's where I probably seen you before. My name's Mico. Mico Brunson."

"I'm Rudolph. Rudolph Henry. They call me Rudy."

"This is my potna, DJ, from North Carolina."

We exchanged daps and went to Rudy's apartment to call the police. His apartment was nicely decorated as if he had a woman living with him. It was equipped with all new furniture and appliances. He gave us a thorough run down on the D.C. scene, including the apartment complex that we were living in. Apparently, we chose to live in one of the most drug-infested areas in Southern Maryland. It really didn't bother me as much as it did DJ. He felt real uncomfortable after Rudy finished his stories about D.C. Rudy had plenty of stories to tell and he told them in true Texan fashion, complete with every syllable drawn out with an extra twang. He even gave us a run down of his life and how he'd ended up in D.C. I don't know if a lot of it was true, but it sure was entertaining.

"Ya'll want some more beer?" asked Rudy.

"Yeah, I'll take another," I said, as I finished off the beer I had in my hand. "I'm trying to get my mind off of my car."

"Well, shiiiit, I got something to take your mind off of that," Rudy said as he pulled a box off the top of his refrigerator. "After you take a hit of this Texas sting, all your worries will be behind you."

He reached into the box, pulled out a thick joint, and handed it to me.

"Sorry, potna, I don't smoke," I said as I handed the joint to DJ. "But he does."

"Hell yeah," said DJ as he fiddled for his lighter. "Mico only messes with that white girl, but I'll take this fatty for a ride."

"Oh yeah, well I got that too," Rudy said as he dug into his back pocket and flipped a small white packet to me.

"Now you're talkin' my language." I grabbed the white packet, rolled up a dollar bill, and went to work.

For a brief moment, I did something that I had never done before; I let my guard down. I didn't even know Rudy, but his hospitality and demeanor was genuine. It was like we'd known each other for years. At no point did I ever think he was setting us up for something or trying to take advantage of a vulnerable situation. He was cool as hell, and DJ felt the same way. We stayed in his apartment for hours drinking, smoking, snorting, and telling our life stories. Our lives were similar. We grew up poor, were raised by single mothers, and joined the military to get away from it all. The time passed so fast that I forgot to call the cops to report my car stolen.

"Oh shit, I forgot to call the cops."

"Don't worry about it, dog," said Rudy. "I can take you to the substation up the block."

We all hopped into Rudy's work van and went to the substation. After I filed the police report, we went cruising around town. Rudy became a good friend and the work van became our mode of transportation. We would take it everywhere—to clubs, parties, on dates. We had no shame in our game when it came to getting from point A to point Z. Rudy had a good relationship with the owner of the construction company that he worked for.

They were actually involved in more activities than construction. Rudy's boss was connected to the underground powder pipeline. He was moving heavy weight between D.C. and Miami and using the construction company for cover. Rudy's job was to step on the powder and pass it to their connection in Virginia.

The Hustle Continues

After hanging out with Rudy for a while, he let me in on the operation because, even though DJ and I got the job we wanted with the investment company, we were only making pennies while going through their training program. Rudy agreed to pinch some cocaine off the shipments he was stepping on and rock it up so that I could sell the rocks on our block.

I wasn't a two-bit street hustler, never was and didn't want to be, but I had to do something to make a little more money. The pay we were getting from the investment company barely covered our rent and travel expenses. Rudy was cool about it and didn't tax me at all for the rocks he fronted me because he wanted to test the waters.

DJ didn't want to get involved with selling drugs, so he got a part-time job at a neighborhood grocery store. That worked out because we never went hungry. We ate steak and grilled out on the back stoop every weekend. With DJ working at the store, we never ran low on the essentials like toothpaste, soap, and, toilet paper.

I was very nervous about hitting the block at first because I wasn't from the area and I knew how territorial the drug slinging business was. During the late eighties, everybody was selling crack, so the block was saturated with two-bit drug dealers who, at first, really didn't notice I was there. I made sure I stayed in one area and didn't stray out of my territory. I definitely didn't rush cars like over half of the fools out there. That wasn't my style. I stayed perched on a wooden fence and my prospective clients came to me. I would sling drugs all night and get up early in the morning to take the bus and subway to work. After a while, the guys on the block started noticing my pattern and gave me the nickname nine-to-five.

Eventually, the block got real hot and everybody who was out in the open was getting picked off one by one by the Jump Outs. The Jump Outs were a team of undercover cops who rode around drug-infested areas in a black van and would jump out of the van to surprise and roundup the drug dealers. One night, the Jump Outs rolled through our area and all the drug dealers scattered except for a few hard-core dealers who thought they were safe because they kept their stash stuffed in the bricks on the side of the building. But this time, the Jump Outs had drug sniffing dogs with them. They used them to check the cars and the buildings that were near the dealers. I didn't want to move from my spot because it would draw attention to me. I just stayed perched on the fence and watched the show.

The Jump Outs were cuffing the dealers and throwing them in the van. I just knew this would be the night I got caught. I braced myself for the worse. Sure enough, a Jump Out started walking in my direction with one of the dogs. Knowing that I had six vials of crack stuffed in the the fence, I didn't move. I just looked at him as he walked in my direction. He took one look at me, suddenly grabbed his radio, snatched the dog, and quickly ran back to the van. My heart almost exploded. If I got caught, that would mean that all the negative predictions my mother used to make regarding how my life would turn out would come true. If arrested, I would wind up a nobody with a police record and my options for success would be limited.

I snapped out of it and went back to my apartment, leaving the vials of crack in the fence. After I returned to my apartment, I thought long and hard about a plan for my life and realized that I had an opportunity to make something out of myself by using my hustling skills on the job at the investment company.

From that point forward, I vowed not to take any more risks with my life street hustling and to learn as much as I could about investment banking.

After talking to myself for hours and working through my plan, I remembered that I had left the vials of crack in the fence. I started thinking what might happen if some kids found them while they were playing outside the next day. I had to go back and get them.

As I approached the fence, I noticed a couple of images in my peripheral vision walking toward me. It turned out to be Loke, the neighborhood thug, and his crew.

"Whatup youngin?" asked Loke.

"Nada, what's up with you?" I responded.

"You, that's what up with me. Why you didn't get swept with those other fools?"

"Dunno. Got lucky I guess."

"Lucky, my ass. I saw the Jump Outs talking to you. You some kinda narc?."

"Get the fuck outta here. A narc? I'm far from that, potna."

Loke moved closer, and I knew that he would probably try to throw a punch. I braced myself and prepared for battle on the inside. Because I grew up with people like Loke, I knew punks like him always wanted to prove a point. I surveyed the area, looking for something I could use as a weapon because I knew that I would probably get jumped by him and his crew. I didn't have any backup because DJ and Rudy were out running the streets. I noticed a bulge under Loke's shirt, around his waistband area. It looked like the butt of a gun, so I stopped moving toward the fence and got prepared to defend myself.

"Yeah nigga, a narc. I saw the Jump Outs roll up on you, and they didn't even fuck with you. Why is that?"

"Like I said, I got lucky."

"Well your luck just ran out, nigga. Now flip your pockets."

I didn't know what I was most angry about, Loke calling me a narc or him trying to rob me. I had to think quick on my feet. I went for the bulge in his shirt and, luckily, it was a gun. I snatched the gun out of his waistband with my right hand and with one swift motion, knocked him out with a left cross. It all happened so fast that his crew didn't know how to react. They saw the gun in my hand and immediately stepped back. I didn't point the gun in their direction because I knew if anybody moved I would have pulled the trigger.

Not knowing if the gun was loaded, I kept it aimed to the sky.

"Somebody better get this motherfucker out of my face," I said as I placed my back on the fence. I didn't want anyone to get behind me. I learned that lesson the hard way.

Luckily, no one in his crew had a gun. I think they were more awed by seeing their boy getting knocked out cold. Loke was supposed to be one of the toughest guys on the block. He got a boost to his reputation after he pistol-whipped one of the neighborhood drug dealers a week prior with the same pistol I was waving in the air. His reputation as the toughest guy on the block was in jeopardy because now his crew had to scrape his ass off the concrete.

After the altercation with Loke, all the thugs and drug dealers on the block gave me much respect and gave me props every time they saw me. Even though I wore a shirt and tie every day to work, they knew that "nine to five" was no punk. I stopped hustling on the block, but that didn't stop me from hanging out with the hustlers after work. I would get in a couple of games of craps or just pop a forty ounce and talk about crazy shit. They used to always like for me to talk about my experience in the military and all the international women I spoiled. As for Loke, he wasn't allowed to come on our block anymore. I had to watch my back for a little while because he was the retaliation type, but I didn't have to watch for long because he disappeared in the system for beating his live-in girlfriend to death.

Moving on Up

DJ and I stayed in the hood for about a year before making enough money to move to a three-bedroom apartment in a better area. Rudy moved in with us. He and his boss eventually stopped moving drugs between Miami and Virginia because they won a major government contract that kept the work steady. They decided to concentrate more on growing their construction business, rather than their drug business.

I was making notable strides hustling on my job at the investment company, building a portfolio of serious clients. The work environment was real stressful at times because of the quotas. Management was a stickler on the brokers meeting their quotas and, if they didn't, they were out the door in a heartbeat. It was a high-pressured environment, but my supervisor was laid back and very helpful. He was a superstar in the company, and he vowed to help me get to superstar status. The job actually came easy to me because convincing people to invest money into pipe dreams was a lot like hustling. It was even better than street hustling because I didn't have to put up any money. I used other people's money to pay for other people ideas. It was kind of weird for me in the beginning, but it turned out to be a great way to make a living.

In the beginning, DJ was doing better than I was. He landed a couple of big-time clients who had lots of money to burn and, with his gift of gab, he was able to get more money out of his clients than the normal broker. He was the talker, and I was more of a doer. In any case, we were both experiencing positive success and it felt good. Life was looking up for all of us. Rudy was now a partner in his construction firm, and DJ and I were on our way to master broker status. We still didn't have enough to buy the type of cars we thought we deserved and while other young professionals were driving their BMWs and Mercedes to the clubs, we still drove the construction van. It really didn't matter to us because we knew that eventually we would be "rolling Kilo G" as we called it.

DJ landed another whale of a client and was quickly recognized by management as a rising star. To celebrate, we decided to go out to the most popular club in the city—the Ritz—and, as usual, we drove the construction van. We could've caught a cab but didn't want to waste our liquor money on a cab ride. We parked the van around the corner and strolled up to the club like high rollers. The Ritz was the happening spot and packed as usual. It had four floors with each floor playing different music: House, Hip Hop, R&B, and Reggae. I liked Reggae a lot, so I convinced the guys to follow me.

All the women in the club were gorgeous as hell. I couldn't believe the sight of so many fine-ass women in one place. We started acting like kids in a candy store. I was confident that with DJ's debonair demeanor and Rudy's Texas twang, we would definitely be going home with a couple dimes. We finally made it to the Reggae club, ordered some champagne, and toasted all of our success.

The night was full of drinking, fun, and dirty dancing with beautiful women. We roamed the different clubs for a while and eventually got separated. I made it back to the Reggae club because that's where I felt most comfortable. Besides, it satisfied my taste for exotic-looking women.

While ordering another drink at the bar, I thought I recognized a woman sitting across the bar. From a distance, she looked like Jasmine. I had to get a closer look. I paid for my drink and moved in for a better look and, to my surprise, it was her. Some guy was hovering over her, whispering in her ear. I started to interrupt, but contained my excitement and moved closer so that she could see me. I wanted to see how she would react or if she would even recognize me.

Suddenly, I felt the guy she was talking to bump up against me as if he were pushed and felt her arms wrap around my neck followed by those soft lips I remembered so vividly, pressed against my cheeks. I turned to her and returned the kiss on her cheeks, which quickly turned into a passionate kiss on the lips. I kept one eye open just in case the guy she pushed away had any issues that needed to be addressed.

"Oh my god," screeched Jasmine. "It's you. It's my baby! I can't believe it!"

"I am in shock right now," I replied. "I am at a loss for words. I just want to hold you."

We stood there and held each other for what seemed an eternity. She smelled so good that I wanted her in a bad way right there and she wanted me. She was even more beautiful than what I remembered.

Running into Jasmine at that time in my life was fate at its best. We could have stayed there forever, holding each other. After our long embrace, we finally wiped our eyes and found a quiet place to catch up. We talked, kissed, and held each other for the rest of the night. I had forgotten all about DJ and Rudy, that is, until they finally found me.

They didn't realize that Jasmine was someone from my past. I remember mentioning her to DJ and even showing him pictures several times but the alcohol consumed his memory.

"What up, man?" says Rudy. "We've been lookin' for you all night."

"Damn, now I see why you got lost," chimed DJ as he admired Jasmine's beauty.

"She accosted me and won't let me go," I remarked.

"You got that right," said Jasmine as she placed a passionate kiss on my lips.

"Damn!" DJ and Rudy said.

"I guess this means you're not rolling with us," says Rudy.

Jasmine looked into my eyes as if to say "hell no," then grabbed my hands and placed them on her thighs. She started kissing me on my neck and licking me behind my ears.

"Uh, I don't think so, fellas," I responded. "Don't worry, I'll make it home. I'm in good hands."

And with a big smile on my face, I brushed them off with a wave of the hand.

In Too Deep

I spent the rest of the weekend with Jasmine at her place. She took me on a shopping spree and filled me in on what her life was like in New York taking care of her mother. She told me that her brother and uncle had come from Jamaica to help, but she later found out that her brother had other motives.

She said that he would spend hours down in the basement with his Jamaican friends. At first, she didn't know what was going on because he wouldn't allow anyone in the basement and would always keep a lock on the door when he left the house. But after their mother's doctors' bills grew to a point where her insurance stopped paying and they couldn't afford the bills, he finally showed her what he was doing in the basement.

He was using the house as a manufacturing plant for crack. He and his crew had manufactured tons of it in the basement and had a plan to starting selling kilos of cocaine already in crack form. This was something that no other crew was doing at the time. The plan was to blanket the city with a large volume of it and fill the void where other crews couldn't keep up with the demand. They anticipated that the street distributors would rather deal with them because the hard work had already been done. Their plan worked.

Using this strategy, the Jamaican Posse was born. They were a ruthless bunch that infiltrated and cornered the drug market in New York and New Jersey in no time. Jasmine had no idea that her mother's house was being used as the major hub for their drug activity right under her nose. Her brother was a lieutenant in the organization and ran a tight ship. She told me that, after seeing all the crack lining the basement walls up to the ceiling, she had no choice but to help her brother move it. Besides, her mother's life depended on it. Jasmine felt that her involvement was the only way she could pay for her mother's cancer treatments.

"There's no getting out," said Jasmine. "It's like the mafia. Once you are tied up in this mess, you can't just walk away."

"But he's your brother," I said. "Can't he just let you walk away?"

"I know too much, and now I'm running stuff between New York and D.C."

"That's crazy to put your little sister in harm's way for your own financial gain."

"Oh, he pays me well and I have no regrets because I did it for my mother, but the more trips I make, the more risky it becomes."

"How many runs are you making?"

"I'm up to two a week."

"Well," I paused. "Excuse me for asking, but what's the take?"

"I don't care about you asking. You know you can ask me anything. I get five grand per run."

"Five grand? Damn, that's a lot of loot."

A part of me wanted to press the issue because I wanted in, but another part of me was telling myself to walk away and fast because, although the money seemed good, it would eventually lead to a dead end. Unfortunately, my method of operation was to always go with my first intuition and wanting in was my first intuition.

"Sounds like you need a little help," I said.

Jasmine didn't respond immediately. She just lay there, curled up next to me, staring at me with those big brown eyes.

"I do need someone to help me get away from this mess, but I don't want that person to be you."

"This is at least something I'm good at. I practically invented the art. Hell, I was doing that type of shit when I was eleven. I didn't get caught then, and I won't get caught now."

"If I bring you in, and you get wrapped up in it, you can't get out."

"Don't worry about me. I'm just worried about getting you out of it."

Even though my life was finally on the right track with a good job that was turning into a career, I still yearned for the excitement of making fast money. Besides, it could only get me closer to my dream. The excitement of the underworld kept my adrenaline pumping, and it was where I felt most comfortable.

Having a corporate job was also exciting, especially with what I was involved in, which, in my eyes, was legal gambling. I became comfortable in the boardroom, presenting my portfolio to the big dogs. The only drawback was the corporate politics, which sometimes overwhelmed my desire to continue. The money was steady, but not enough to help me get to my goal. Jasmine's way would get me there much faster.

We went on to discuss how we would approach her brother about bringing me into his crew. All I needed was to clear about one hundred thousand dollars, and I could put a down payment on my first apartment complex. With Jasmine back in my life, I just knew life couldn't be more perfect.

Just like old times, Jasmine and I spent every free moment together. If I wasn't working, I was with her. If she wasn't doing her thing, she was with me. My nights were her nights and her days were my days. Rudy and DJ would often tease me about the time I was spending with Jasmine, but every time they saw her, they understood why.

Jasmine knew I wasn't happy with my job. She knew I was out of my element working a nine-to-five gig but she respected the fact that I would do just about anything it took to survive. She knew I had a plan and wanted to help me achieve it in any way she could.

We opened a bank account together to start saving money for my dream, which eventually turned into our dream. I even took some of the money and pumped it into some volatile stock that I was tracking. I was able to flip five grand into twenty-five grand in two weeks. Jasmine was so impressed with what I was able to do with the money, she wanted to give me more to flip but I convinced her to be patient. I was more cautious with our money than I was with any of my clients'. After a while, money wasn't a factor at all for us. We made lots of it, spent lots of it, and saved some.

One week, Jasmine went missing for three days straight without contacting me, and I wasn't able to contact her. Those three days felt like an eternity. I knew she was making one of her runs, but that usually took no longer than eight hours. This time her absence seemed unusually long and unbearable. Every bad thought I could think of ran through my mind from her being jacked, in a car crash, to her getting locked up. I remember saying to myself that if she didn't contact me by the end of the fourth day, I was going to go to New York to look for her. I certainly didn't know where I would start but I didn't care, either.. Then the phone on my desk rang.

"Hello," I answered.

"Baby?" said Jasmine on the other end. "Come down, I want to take you to lunch."

"Where have you been?"

"I will explain when I see you."

Wasting no time, I made a mad dash to the elevators and, when I reached the parking lot, I noticed her sitting on the hood of a shiny new sports car. It was a Nissan 300 Z, which was my dream car at the time. She threw me the keys and jumped into my arms.

"Baby, I've missed you," she said as she blanketed me with kisses.

"Damn, where have you been?" I asked. "You can't leave me like that without calling. My heart can't take it. I was worried about you."

"I know you were, but I couldn't call. Get in and take me for a spin in your new car. I'll tell you all about my adventure."

I was shocked and excited that she bought me a new car, but I was also concerned that she was in too deep. As we drove around, she told me of her trip to Jamaica and how spiritual it was as well as financially rewarding. Apparently, she was able to transport a large amount of cocaine into the United States. The amount of money she made in three days was more than I made in a year.

She started spending money like water and most of the time she spent it on me. I became very concerned, and I knew I had to do something to get her out of the game. Even though her brother was a leader in the Jamaican Posse, I feared for her safety because anything could happen. There were a lot of murders happening as a result of the crack craze and most of it was because of the Posse.

During the early nineties, they were one of the most ruthless drug factions around. They controlled the drug world in New York and New Jersey with a reputation of brutality and forceful vengeance. Their trademark was death to their enemies by machete.

After cornering the market up north, they ventured south into D.C., Virginia, and even North Carolina. Using the same fear tactics, they attempted to take control of the drug scene in D.C. but met a level of resistance they weren't ready for. The drug dealers in D.C. were just as ruthless and they weren't backing down. Southeast D.C., Southern Maryland, and Northern Virginia became fierce battlegrounds.

After a few months passed, and I still hadn't met with Jasmine's brother, I was concerned that she didn't want to go through with it, so I decided to show up unannounced at her apartment one Sunday. I remember her telling me that her brother came over every Sunday to count his money and to regroup. I wanted to make my surprise visit seem genuine, so I picked up some flowers and her favorite candy on the way over to her place.

As I turned the corner on her block, I ran into a squad of police cars crowding the street in front of her apartment building. My first instinct was to throw my car in reverse and get the hell out of there, but it hit me. For the first time in my life, I was legitimate. The car wasn't stolen, I had insurance, and my driver's license was in order. I parked the car in the first available space and attempted to get out to see what was going on. But before I had a chance to open the driver's door, a cop approached and blocked my exit.

"Sir, you can't park here right now."

"What's going on?"

"We have a crime scene here. You can't park here. Move it now."

I didn't bother pressing the issue. I got out of there as fast as I could without drawing too much attention to myself. I definitely didn't want to be associated with any crime scene. On my way home, I pulled over to call Jasmine from a pay phone. There was no answer. I tried calling her on her car phone, but still no answer. I hopped back in my car and decided to drive around for a while. I figured the cops would clear out eventually, so I just wanted to buy some time. I stopped every thirty minutes to call Jasmine. Several hours passed, and I still hadn't heard a word from her.

Finally, after I couldn't stand it anymore, I became concerned and went back to her apartment. It was well into the night when I returned, but after seeing the number of police that remained in front of her apartment building, I decided to go home. Again, I stopped several times and tried contacting her. I then thought maybe she was being blocked from entering her apartment or from getting to her car, so I rushed to get home just in case she was trying to call me.

I returned to my apartment and was immediately met by DJ and Rudy. Rudy seated in the kitchen and DJ on the couch. The look from both of them was eerie and solemn.

"Jasmine call?" I asked, tossing my keys on the coffee table.

The silence from DJ and Rudy was deafening, as their eyes remained glued to the television. Then suddenly, a nod from DJ directed my attention to the television. As I looked, I caught a brief image of my Jasmine followed by disturbing commentary. She had been brutally murdered in her apartment along with two men of Jamaican descent.

A sharp pain rushed through my body and paralysis set in. My mind went totally blank. DJ and Rudy attempted to console me. Rudy even hugged me, but I couldn't feel anything.

Consumed with anger, sadness, denial, and revenge, I was on exile in my room for three days. DJ and Rudy left me alone. I didn't eat or drink anything. I can't remember if I even used the bathroom.

"C'mon, baby boy," Rudy yelled from other side of my door. "I'm not going to let you stay in there any longer. You gotta get over this. I'm rolling to the store and when I get back, I'm coming in to get you."

Rudy's words broke me out of my three-day trance, I reached for my gun, the same gun I took from Loke. It was cocked and loaded. I disengaged it and emptied all the bullets on the bed. After double-checking the barrel to ensure no bullet was left in the chamber, I placed the barrel of the gun to my head. I told myself that if I could pull the trigger, it would prove that I had no purpose to live. I tried and tried, but couldn't pull the trigger.

A force came over me as I glared at the makeshift shrine of Jasmine on my dresser. The candles had burned out, but the rays of the sun glistened off her eyes in the photo. I finally came to grips with my loss. I had to move on. I'd been through too much in my life to let something like this take me out.

Making a Comeback

I regained my senses and my strength, packed my bags, and headed to the only place I would find solace, my Aunt Lucy's house. It'd been years since I'd been back to Detroit, and I didn't know what to expect upon my return. It really didn't matter to me because my destination wasn't Detroit, it was my Aunt Lucy's house. I had no plans of returning to my old neighborhood, I just wanted to see my aunt; nothing else mattered. I knew she could ease my pain.

As soon as I hit her block, I could smell the aroma of a home-cooked meal seeping out of Aunt Lucy's kitchen window. It was as if she knew I was coming. Without knocking, I unlatched the screen door from the outside as only I knew how.

"Auntie?" I yelled from the foyer so that I wouldn't startle her too much.

"Mico?" she responded from the kitchen without looking to see if it was me. "Baby, is that you?"

I rushed to the kitchen and was met with the snuggle hug that I desperately needed. Her embrace was as warm as I remembered it to be and, all of a sudden, my problems seemed to subside as they had in the past. My mind and heart were at ease and the tears finally flowed because I knew she would catch them.

"It's okay, baby. Go ahead and cry. It's healthy and you'll feel better when you're through."

"It hurts so much. What did I do to deserve this type of life?"

"It will be all right. These things happen. It's not just your life. It's life in general. We gotta accept the bad with the good."

"It's so hard, Auntie."

"I know, baby. That's what I'm here for."

With that, a smile graced my face and the relief replaced the grief. The only unconditional love I'd ever received in life came from my Aunt Lucy. I was home again and I was safe. Although, I knew she didn't know the details of what was weighing heavily on my heart, she knew and felt my pain; therefore, all she had to do was hold me.

"Wipe your eyes, baby, and put your bags in your room so you can come and get something to eat."

She didn't have to tell me twice. Before she could blink an eye, I was at the kitchen table ready to devour a good home-cooked meal, a definite change from the burger diet I was accustomed to. We talked well into the night. I could always talk to her about anything and, even after several years of separation, our relationship was no different.

Although, I didn't miss anything about my old neighborhood nor did I want to return, I just knew my trip wouldn't have been complete unless I paid a visit. The psychological wounds were still fresh, but I figured the only way to bring closure to a part of my life that I wasn't proud of was to go back.

Fifteen years had passed since I stepped foot on my old street. My old house was no longer there. The city had torn down the homes and replaced them with a townhouse community for low-income families. Our old headquarters were also gone, but the elementary school was still there; it seemed smaller than I remembered. As I approached the school, memories of my dad emerged and his image became more vivid when I placed my hand on the fence that surrounded the schoolyard. To make my visit complete, I had to find out what happened to Man Man. My aunt knew where his mother lived, so I drummed up the courage and decided to pay her a visit. She still lived on the Eastside.

When I approached her house, I saw a figure sitting on the porch in a wheelchair. As I got closer, the face became familiar. It was Man Man. A lump lodged in my throat at the thought that it was probably my fault he was in a wheelchair. I didn't know where my bullets landed the day I fired at Jeff. I braced myself for retaliation and ridicule because I deserved it.

"Mico?" he called before I placed my foot on the first step.

"Man Man?" I responded.

"Oh my dear Jesus."

The reference to Jesus startled me a bit. This definitely wasn't the Man Man I once knew.

"Yeah, it's me."

"Oh my God, you still alive? This is a blessing. Give me love," he said as he extended his arms.

His mother appeared at the front door, shook her head, and disappeared back into the house.

"Yeah, Man, I'm still here"

We engaged in an apprehensive embrace.

"Don't let it scare you, brother. I'm still alive."

Suddenly, the images flashed through my mind of the last day I saw him being pummeled by Jeff. I finally had my answer. I found out what happened to the bullets. But before I became overwhelmed with grief, Man Man explained how he wound up in the wheelchair.

"The cops did this to me, bro. They raided one of our camps. We all ran, but I got caught jumping over a fence."

"They shot you in the back?"

"Naw, this cop threw his night stick and it hit me in the lower back, cracking my spine."

"Damn. What a freak accident."

"Yeah, it made me a freak, but that's me. What's been up with you? I'm really shocked to see you alive."

We spent the rest of the day catching up with each other's lives. Man Man gave me the run down on the whole crew. Most of them killed or in jail. David was serving three life sentences for murders they pinned on the organization. Apparently, an undercover snitch infiltrated YHI and caused its implosion. David lost his edge and started doing more drugs than he was selling. The authorities raided all the YHI camps and yielded the biggest drug and illegal arms bust in the history of the city. I didn't ask about Jeff. I didn't care to know nor did Man Man care to tell me.

My trip back to Detroit proved to be therapeutic. Visiting my aunt and all the old places I used to roam provided the closure and inspiration that I needed, especially seeing Man Man and knowing that he didn't catch one of the bullets meant for Jeff. Now it was time for me to grow up and move on with my life and my career.

Mastering the Corporate Hustle

After spending a week in Detroit, I returned to D.C. and submerged myself in my work. I gave up partying and cut down on liquor and drug consumption. My memories of Jasmine remained, but I learned to control my emotions and moved on. I started gaining ground on DJ's success at the office and upper management started to notice my accomplishments. All it took was landing a couple of whales to pad my portfolio and my career took off. Soon I was considered for the Leadership Advancement Program, which placed me on to track to becoming a master broker, which was the aspiration of all junior brokers.

As part of the program, I was assigned a mentor. By the luck of the draw, I presumed, Carl Mabon, a master broker and the son of one of the firm's owners, was assigned to me. He was a smooth brother who came to work sharp every day, decked out in five-hundred-dollar suits, complimented with expensive shoes. It was obvious that being the son of the owner had its perks, but as I quickly found out, his desire to succeed surpassed any nepotistic characteristics.

Carl had been with the firm from its inception and his experience was unparalleled. Before he helped his father create the company, he worked for one of the largest investment firms on Wall Street. He was the top producer in the company and became a self-made millionaire before he turned twenty-five.

He and I connected almost immediately and, for six weeks, I did nothing but shadow his every move. In the boardroom, on client calls, and during business meetings, I was there watching him operate. His style was unlike anything I'd experienced. Even the top hustlers in the hood would be amazed by his negotiation skills. I was most impressed at how he handled his business in front of the powerful white millionaires and billionaires. He would make them feel that what they'd done in the past to acquire their wealth was nothing compared to the amount of money that our company could make them with a few wise investments. His moves were poetic.

I was awestruck with his style so much that I ate, slept, dreamt, and breathed Carl and, after a while, I became him. It wasn't long before I started making the money commensurate to my dedication. The money started rolling in along with the corporate perks and, within one year, I was considered a major player. All eyes were on me. The attention felt good, but the adrenaline felt even better. I took my hustle to another level and there was no looking back.

I began spending less time with DJ and Rudy. DJ and I would have lunch together from time to time but even that faded as I began spending more time with Carl. As for Rudy, he became involved with a girl who kept him hostage at her place in Virginia most of the time. The landscape of my life was changing and I welcomed the change.

"The big man is impressed, bro," said Carl one day as he leaned back in his retro-Italian leather chair, propping his feet up on his mahogany-trimmed desk.

"All in a day's work, my brother," I said as I slumped back from a long day of negotiating a major investment deal.

"You're on fire, man. You remind me of me when I was coming up sparring with those white boys on Wall Street."

"I had an outstanding teacher."

"Well I can't argue with that."

We both laughed at his arrogance.

"Hey, what's on your agenda for the weekend?" asked Carl, lighting up one of his Cuban cigars.

"Work as usual, my brother."

"Work? Naw, not this weekend, bro."

"Man I gotta stay sharp. I can't let up or the next man will take my spot."

"Hell," he laughed. "You've left so much distance between you and the next man that it'll take years to catch up."

"Well, this is true."

"Give it a break this weekend, my man. The old man wanted me to invite you to one of his Big Dog parties to celebrate your success."

"Big Dog party?"

"Yeah, this is where he invites all of the company's top clients and they're supposed to bring at least one of their wealthy acquaintances."

"Sounds like work to me."

"Well, you're right, but the playing field is a little different. Besides, in our line of work, the hustle never ends."

He was right. The hustle never ended, especially when you were on top of your game. You had to keep the momentum going. By being invited to the big guy's party, I felt I had finally made it to the big league. I had a nice stash in the bank, had one foot out of the hood, and was finally on the right track to accomplishing my dream. Oddly, everything seemed to be working out a little too well. It actually started to scare me a little because my mother always said that, "a horse runs fast but they don't run long." But I decided not to let the anxiety of my success take control of me, so I took hold of the reins and vowed to enjoy the ride.

The day of the party, I bought a new suit and a new pair of shoes so that I would appear fresh and clean for my potential clients. All day I prepped my pitch and introduction. My strategy was to design the pitch to seem like a regular conversation, subtle, yet enticing. The big guy didn't want the party to seem like it was a setup to generate new business, even though it was. He billed it as an appreciation gathering for the company's top clients. As the new guy on the block, I certainly didn't want to appear like a salesman because I would stand out like a sore thumb.

As I approached the big guy's house, I started feeling inadequate as I passed a collage of high-priced luxury cars with my used low-end sports car. Although, I wasn't a materialistic person, the thought did cross my mind that maybe it was time for me to step up my game. I deserved it, and I definitely could afford it. But, upgrading my car before I upgraded to a new house, seemed asinine. I couldn't afford to upgrade to a fifteen-bedroom mansion with the five-acre manicured lawn like the big guy, but I could at least afford a townhouse or a condo in a upscale neighborhood. This was something I had to work on, but it had to wait until after the party and after I bagged a couple more whales.

"There he is," Carl exclaimed as he approached me in the foyer. "My protégé!"

He gave me the drink that he had been sipping on.

"Drink up, partner," he whispered. "We got a lotta fishing to do and, believe me, they're biting. It must be the good liquor."

I sucked the drink down and quickly got into hustle mode. Carl was right. All the players were there and they brought along some prime prospects. I don't know if it was the adrenaline or the desire, but I bounced from prospect to prospect, bagging each one. I was on a role and every thing I had planned to say, came out flawlessly. They knew that I knew the business because I had the portfolio of clients and stocks to prove it.

A couple of hours into the party, I decided to take a breather and stepped out on the patio. I thought I would be able relax and collect my thoughts before returning to the party to bag more whales, but before I could get settled, Carl approached me with a very pleasant package on his arm.

"Mico, I would like for you to meet a very dear friend of mine. This is Talia."

"Hello, Mico. Carl has told me a lot about you."

"Really?" I said. "Well, he has managed to keep you a secret, and I see why."

"Well, she is my secret," said Carl as he pulled her close and placed a kiss on her cheek. "My secret weapon, that is."

"I guess every good man should have one," I chuckled.

"Well, she could be yours too."

"Wow, is it that easy for you to just give me away like that?" Talia responded jokingly.

"Only for a couple of minutes, babe."

He released her hand and gestured that I should pick up where he left off.

Without hesitation, I immediately took her hand.

"Wow, how can a man in his right mind give up a woman like you?"

"I dunno. I keep asking myself the same thing. It must be the wooden leg."

I quickly looked away as not to allow myself to look at her legs, but couldn't keep my eyes off of her smooth pecan-colored skin, coupled with a smile that could light up the Holland Tunnel. All complimented by her model-like figure atop her thin but shapely five-foot-seven frame. I really wasn't into thin frames, but she wore hers well.

"I don't have a wooden leg," she said with a burst of laughter. "You can look at them."

We both laughed.

After the icebreaker, we talked and laughed well into the night. I forgot about the other whales that needed to be bagged at the party because Talia, to me, was the ultimate catch. I was relieved when she told me how she and Carl knew each other.

It turned out that they weren't an item at all. They actually grew up together in the same neighborhood and had been classmates through high school. They went to separate colleges but, because they had become such good friends growing up, they stayed in touch. Carl was actually madly in love with Talia's best friend, Gina, who was also at the party. So Carl, as slick as he was, managed to pawn Talia off on me so that he could spend more time with Gina alone, which of course, I didn't regret.

We tuned everyone out at the party as we talked and laughed the night away. Before we knew it, everyone had left and the sun was peaking in on our side of the world once again.

"Oh my goodness," Talia squelched as she noticed the sun coming up. "Where did the time go?"

"That's funny. I thought that time stood still."

"Now that was real corny. Ah man, you were doing so well."

"Damn, it was kind of corny? It's too late or too early, depending on how you look at it."

With that, we decided to call it a night but vowed to meet up again for dinner.

After walking her to her car, I returned to what I thought was an empty house to catch a couple of hours of sleep on the couch before driving home. Before I could close my eyes, Carl emerged; his shirt unbuttoned with blue silk boxer shorts and mixed-matched socks.

"Damn, man, your socks mess up your whole ensemble"

"Never mind my socks. What about Talia?"

"She is fine as hell, you know that. But what's her story?"

"She's single and prime for the picking, my friend."

"How does a girl like that stay single? Something must be wrong with her."

"Naw, it's her job. She's a public relations manager for the Bullets and she's always on the road, hanging around shallow-ass men with big egos. That type of atmosphere thickened her skin a bit, but I'm sure a smooth brother like you can soften it up."

"You punk, did you just play matchmaker?"

"Naw, my brother, I just saw an emerging opportunity and connected the dots."

"Always working, aren't you?"

"Always, bro, always."

"There's gotta be something about her that you are not telling me."

"Not really. She's a lifelong friend and a great business partner."

"A business partner? How so?"

"Let's just say that she is my claim to fame. Everyone has to have that edge and she was mine for a long time."

Carl sat on the couch beside me a let me in on how he shot to the top of his game using Talia.

Apparently, Talia was heavy into the club scene while she was in college. She promoted parties for the popular athletes from colleges in Washington, D.C., Virginia, North Carolina, and even New York. Her popularity was huge. Most of the college athletes she knew turned pro and eventually became rich. Since Carl was a struggling broker looking for whales to bag, Talia would connect him to the rich athletes she knew. Then, like a tiny snowball rolling down a snow-capped mountain, through word of mouth and a few smart investment leads, Carl's portfolio grew larger than life.

"We were the perfect tag team," said Carl. "She would bag them and I would tag them. The fun part was that it was a win–win situation for everyone involved. Everyone got paid. Everyone got fat and happy."

"But?" I questioned.

"No buts, bro. She still feeds me today. Of course, she got out of the party scene, but she is still connected through her PR work with the NBA."

"By the tone of this story, I feel there's a but in there somewhere."

"No buts, bro. It's just that the game has expanded."

White-Collar Criminals

Carl went on to tell me how the game was expanded from just a money-moving business to a money-shuffling one. That most of his millionaire clients were willing to pay significant fees for hiding money from the government and creditors using offshore bank accounts. The money that they saved in taxes, lawsuits from money-grubbing ex-spouses, greedy family members, and ambulance chasers were in the billions. They didn't mind paying significant fees to what Carl called Offshore Account Agents to shuffle and hide their assets.

At first, I thought that it all sounded kind of grimy and illegal, but after Carl convinced me that the middleman wasn't breaking any laws, I decided that I wanted in. I was more impressed than shocked to learn that Carl had created an underground network of offshore account agents and wanted me to join.

After being introduced to a new way of making more money, I was able to learn the ropes. Carl taught me the secret processes and how to use the software to move the funds to and between offshore bank accounts. He used secret numbers and a language that only people in the underground network knew. There were hundreds of fake U.S.-based bank accounts that were set up under fake businesses that were used to transfer funds from the U.S. accounts in the Caribbean and Europe. The electronic transfers were automatically rotated between accounts and masked through heavy encryption methods so that the authorities couldn't intercept or decipher the money transfers. The entire process was complex, but it was designed that way to ensure that the clients or agents wouldn't get tracked or caught. The number-one rule was not to reveal your true identity to your client.

"Honey, are you going to spend any more time with me today before I leave?" interrupted Gina as she peeked her head through the door to the study.

"I'm sorry, baby," responded Carl. "I'll be right there."

"Damn," I gulped. "She is fine as hell. You lucky mother."

"Shut your mouth!"

"I'm just talking 'bout Gina."

We both laughed.

"Check this out," said Carl as he handed me what appeared to be a homemade manual. "Run through the scenario that starts on page sixteen at least five times. After that, you should have a good idea of how it all works. I will get Talia to set you up with your first client. We'll start you off with a small fish and work you up to the big whales. You good?"

"Oh, I'm good," I responded as took the manual and started flipping through the pages. "Go handle your business. I'm real good."

After Carl left the room, I couldn't help but to think how he may have used Talia to soften me up to the idea of joining his private network, but after spending some time with her, it turned out that the matchmaking deal was legitimate.

Talia and I started dating and became intimately close. The relationship became serious enough that, after a couple of months of dating, we decided to move in together.

"I guess this is it, dog," said Rudy as he threw the last piece of my luggage in the back of his van.

"Man, we will still see each other," I said.

"I know, man, but it won't be the same."

"Shit, that's not a bad thing. I guess we're all grown up now."

"I guess you're right. We can't stay po pimps forever."

"When I get all settled in, I'll give you guys a call and we can fire up the grill."

"True dat. Hey, when you finish with the van, just drop the key in the usual spot."

I jumped in the van and headed for the next phase in my life. To be honest, I was ready to settle down. My days of being a playboy and hustler were over. Talia had snagged me hook, line, and sinker. She bagged her whale.

My career was in high gear and the underground network was running flawlessly. It turned out not to be as complex as I'd first thought. The set up was sweet and secure. We took our money off the top for every transaction. I didn't have to worry about calculating the splits between Talia, myself, and Carl because we used a computer application that did it all for us. The trickiest part of the whole operation was secretly making the initial deposit without drawing too much attention. The deposits were usually in the millions and, although our network included a host of bank executives, they sometimes appeared a bit shaky because they really didn't know where the money was coming from. They didn't know if the money was coming from a drug cartel, the mob, a terrorist group, or a legitimate source. Every time we made a deposit, it was always fun to see them turn the other cheek as they crammed thousands of dollars in their pockets.

The money shuffling operation ran smooth and easy. With my involvement, Carl was able to concentrate more on helping his father run the investment company. It really didn't take too much time away from my day-to-day duties. I usually shuffled money for my clients in the evening. I just approached it as a part-time hustle. No one on the job was aware that I was making thousands of dollars a week moving money on the down low. Before I knew it, I had enough money to invest in my first apartment building but decided to wait because I had too much going on, and I would not have been able to manage the property effectively. I kept banking the money instead.

"Baby," Talia whispered in her sexy voice as she curled up beside me in bed. "I need you to meet somebody tomorrow."

"Damn, baby, another prospect?"

"Yeah, but this one is a small timer."

"How so?"

"He's in college right now, but he's the biggest NBA prospect on the market right now."

"Biggest NBA prospect? Who? You're not talking about . . . you can't be talking about Larry Byers from Georgetown are you?"

"Yep, in the flesh."

"How the hell did you bag him?"

"I met his big brother at a conference this week. We started talking about college athletes and how they made so much money for the school but never got to share in the profits. He said his brother was offered a big sum of money under the table but couldn't accept it because he was afraid of getting caught. One thing led to another and—"

"And that's when you kept the door propped opened and reeled his ass in."

"You know it."

"Damn, you're good."

"You know it."

"Yes I do," I said as I grabbed her and kissed her passionately.

The next day we met with Larry Byers over lunch. He told us how the coach and school offered him a million dollars not to go pro until he graduated. He would be a senior next year, so he really didn't want to go pro, but he had so many pro scouts knocking on his door offering him the world. It was getting harder and harder for him to turn them away. If he could accept the money offered by the school, he could help his family and wouldn't give the pro scouts a second look until he graduated.

I agreed to help Larry out for a nominal fee. I didn't charge him my usual rate because I knew he would be back once he turned pro. With a handshake, we clinched the deal.

Larry was a cool kid who was from the rough side of Maryland and had to grow up fast because of his talent. Everyone who met and knew him liked him. We actually clicked from the moment we met and after I moved some money for him, he started inviting me to his basketball games and after parties. I usually accepted his invitations because I wanted to establish a close connection and to gain his trust, not to mention the possibility of meeting more prospects.

After hanging out with Larry for a while, I started seeing some strange behavior. He started disappearing from the after parties more and more and, when he returned, he would seem lethargic and distant. I started to suspect he was doing drugs but would never smell anything on him.

"Yo, dog, are you all right?" I asked while driving Larry home after one of our many after parties.

"Yeah man, I'm cool," he slurred as he leaned back in the passenger seat. "Just get me home safely, man. I'm worth millions you know."

"Yeah, bro, I know. I also think you need to slow down a little and take a break from all this partying."

"Man, I left my mom at home tonight."

"I'm not trying to be your mom. I'm just looking out."

"If you really wanna look out for me, look out for a crackhead so I can get my man done."

"Not tonight, potna. The only crackhead you gonna see tonight will be in your dreams."

Larry passed out before I reached his dorm. I enlisted the help of a couple of guys who were hanging outside of his dorm to help me get him to his room, and I made sure that I locked the door so no one would try to rob him after I left.

I didn't hang out with Larry anymore after that night. Our interactions from that point on were strictly business. I did, however, keep tabs on him from time to time. It seemed the closer he was to inking an NBA deal, the crazier he got. It was almost as if he were scared of success and didn't want to face it head on or sober. He needed help, but I felt he had enough people in his life who could offer the help he needed, so I tuned out.

I kept my mind on climbing the corporate ladder, and soon my hard work paid off. I was appointed Senior VP of Strategic Accounts, assigned to lead a team on structuring an investment deal for none other than David Steiner, my idol. The deal wasn't actually for Mr. Steiner personally, it was for one of his companies. But the thought of inking a deal for a company ran by him was enough to keep me happy for the rest of my career. All I could think about is if I were successful, I could possibly get a chance to meet him in person. I felt like a teenage girl waiting outside a Prince concert. Even though Carl and his dad tagged this whale, I was going to reel it in.

Because of Mr. Steiner's celebrity status, our company was under a microscope. It seemed as though the press followed us to every business meeting in hopes of getting a picture of Mr. Steiner. Every chance Carl got to plug the company, he did. I also took advantage of every photo opportunity, so much so that I wound up in every major business-related magazine on the stands. Even though we were experiencing corporate success, Carl and I continued to operate the underground network because the money was in abundance and it was tax-free.

No More Safety Net

Many months passed before I heard from Larry again. I followed his games and was impressed by the stats he was racking up. He was definitely destined to be the next greatest player ever to hit the NBA.

Out of the blue, the phone rang and it was Larry. He wanted me to meet him at a shopping center near the college. I agreed.

"They ready to make a deal, man," said Larry as he chugged down a cola.

"Who you going with?"

"I don't know yet. The Celtics are offering me the best package so far."

"Celtics are a legendary team. You can't go wrong with them."

"I'm kinda feeling them. They want me to attend their camp this summer."

"Oh man, it sounds like you already in there, but you might want to hold out a little. Make 'em sweat."

"More money, huh man?"

"Money is important, but a solid contract is more important. You want to be covered just in case something happens."

"You're right. That makes a lot of sense. Hell, I should make you my agent."

"I'm already you're agent."

As we both laughed, I could sense there was something else on his mind. I knew he didn't call me there to small talk.

"So what's up, Larry?" I said as I broke up the laughter. "What's on your mind?"

"Damn man, you always about business. You need to lighten up a little."

"I'll lighten up tomorrow. What's up?

"Okay, look, I need to stuff another five hundred thousand."

"Five hundred thousand? You got it on you now?"

"Naw, not right now. I'll have it on Saturday."

"Cool. We'll meet here at two on Saturday."

"Naw, just pick me up from the dorm. We need to roll in the city to pick it up."

"C'mon, Larry, you know it's not my style to spend a lot of time on these deals."

"I know. I know. But I got somebody I want you to meet."

"What?"

"This dude is loaded and we go way back. I told him about you and he wants to use your services. In fact, he needs to use your services before it's too late."

"How much we talkin'?"

"About ten million."

"Ten million?"

"Oh, I got your attention now?"

"With ten million, you can have my bitch."

Larry laughed as I thought to myself that he might be setting me up. But the thought was quickly erased from my mind because I knew Larry wouldn't be smart enough to set me up. Besides, if he did, he would lose over a million dollars that I was shuffling for him, so I bit.

"Okay. I'll pick you up from your dorm at two."

"Cool. You won't regret it. This brother needs to get rid of the money fast."

"If that's the case, then you know I'm the man."

"Yes. You are the man and soon to be my agent."

Larry raised his beer mug as a toast and I obliged.

Although, I hated mysterious meetings, it was how I made my money, through word of mouth among the rich and devious. But something in Larry's eyes bothered me, and I immediately assumed the defensive mode. A little voice in me told me to stand him up on Saturday, but the thought of what my commission would be on ten million dollars kept my interest. The commission from Larry's connection would allow me to step away from the corporate hustle and finally invest in my dream. I had to take the gamble.

Saturday was a stone's throw away from the time I dropped Larry off at his dorm, but quickly became a distant memory after I received a phone call from my mother alerting me to the death of my Aunt Lucy. For a brief moment, I couldn't help but think how my mother probably took pleasure in telling me she was dead. She knew that I loved my Aunt Lucy more than anything in the world and because she was well aware of my success, she took pleasure in seizing the opportunity to bring me pain. My aunt was my only safety net in life and now she was gone at the blink of an eye. Nothing but memories of her generosity and the genuine love she showed me in my times of need filled my every thought. I snapped out of my grief because I didn't want my mother to win by seeing me breakdown at the news.

"When's the funeral?" I asked.

"This Saturday," she responded. "Your brother will be here."

"How did she die? What happened?"

"She died in her sleep. She was old. She died from old age. That's what people do."

I couldn't help but think that my mother was old too and she was still alive. My aunt was a peaceful woman who would never hurt a fly. Why would a sweet and caring person like her die before my mother? It was just another bad hand dealt to me that I would have to deal with, but I couldn't relieve my pain through revenge because she died from natural causes. There was no one to retaliate against, so I had to take it on the chin and keep it bottled up until I found a way to release the pain.

I contacted Larry to let him know I couldn't meet his contact on Saturday due to a death in the family. He said that he would try to set up another meeting, but that his contact was a busy man whose time couldn't be wasted. At this point, it didn't really matter to me, nothing did. I felt numb. Larry just had to find a way to deal with it and make it happen later.

I went back to Port City to attend my aunt's funeral, but not before I bought the car I always wanted, a BMW. Talia and I also went on a shopping spree and bought just about every piece of clothing that had a brand name. I wanted my mother to see, feel, and smell my success. I wanted her to see that the little boy she always said would never amount to anything, made it and made it big.

The funeral was being held in Port City because my mother didn't want to bury my aunt in Detroit. It would've been too far for her to travel to visit and take care of the grave. After the funeral, I spent some time catching up with my brother and few of my cousins but couldn't stay long because I had business to take care of. Talia and I grabbed a hotel room before heading back to D.C. There was no way I was going stay at my mother's place. There were too many bad memories there, and I couldn't hide my disdain for her any longer.

My Past Life Returns

When we returned to D.C., my first order of business was to contact Larry and set up a time that I could meet with his contact.

"You're in luck," Larry said. "He's chillin' at home today, preparing for a trip to New York tomorrow."

"Cool. Set it up," I responded.

"It's already a done deal. I gotta swing by his place this afternoon to pick something up. Just scoop me up at four and we'll roll together."

"I'm there."

This was it, my chance to make a big enough lick to kick off my dream. I remember being anxious all day. I even went to sleep in the middle of the day just to get the chills off me. Talia sensed something was strange about my behavior and came to the lounge room to check on me. She sat down by the couch as she usually did and squeezed the tension out of my shoulders and my back. She didn't say a word, she never did when she knew something was either bothering me or weighing heavy on my mind. That's what I loved about her. She had that sixth sense about her and didn't push any buttons, just let life run its course. I fell asleep from her touch.

When I woke up, my adrenaline was still pumping, but my mind wasn't quite clear. To clear my mind and to kick it into another gear, I had to hit a couple of lines. Cocaine was the great equalizer for me. It didn't matter where I was or what situation I was in, I had to have my stash nearby. As soon as I was done, my mind cleared and it was time for me to take care of business.

I picked up Larry and we headed for his contact's house. The butterflies were fluttering, just as they always did before I embarked on an unknown journey; however, they always flew away when it was time to engage, just like when I used to box.

We approached a modest house in the suburbs just outside of D.C. on the Maryland side. The house appeared to be quite modest for someone who wanted to hide ten million dollars. But it dawned on me that if Larry's contact was a smart man and was involved in criminal activity, then the place was a perfect cover. The thugs perched outside in what appeared to be strategic lookout locations confirmed that Larry's contact wasn't a legitimate business man, so I had to shift into grimy mode.

"What's this, Larry?"

"My man's place."

"You say he got ten million to hide? By the looks of this place, he's hiding it already."

"Yeah, it's a good cover, ain't it?"

"It would be except for the Rolls Royce parked in the driveway."

"Damn man, you sharper than I thought. Look, before we go in there, I just want to give you some ground rules."

"What's that?" I asked.

"He's real temperamental at times, so no wise cracks or quick movements."

"I'm all business, baby, you know that. I don't have time for small talk or ego tripping."

I didn't have to ask Larry what kind of business his contact was into. From the surroundings, I already knew. As we approached the front door to the house, we heard loud voices coming from inside. The closer we got, the louder the voices became, which eventually turned into shouting.

One of the guys who was pacing in front of the front door stopped us from entering. As we stood there, we could here the entire conversation in stereo.

"What the fuck do you mean you got it under control?" said the first voice. "They lifted your fucking fingerprint from the back of that bitch's medallion. Why the fuck didn't you just take the damn medallion?"

"Because it had some bullshit inscription on the back of it and the initials MDB," responded the second voice. "I couldn't give that shit to my girl."

"Well, now you about to give your girl a funeral to go to or a jail to visit. They linked that shit back to you. How long do you think it's gonna take them to link you to me? You're my right hand. God dammit, we planned the perfect hit and one fucking window shopping mistake and we get hemmed the fuck up."

"Stop worrying, E, I'll make this shit disappear. You have my word."

"This shit better disappear."

"It will. I'll use my connections on the force to make it happen."

A burly man rushed out of the door and brushed past us in a hurry. My heart skipped several beats and my knees buckled. I couldn't believe that fate had brought me to the front door of the people who were responsible for Jasmine's death. With the death of my aunt still weighing heavy on my heart and now finding out who killed the love of my life, I was about to explode, but had to regain my composure quickly because all eyes were on me. Unfortunately, I couldn't stop the curl in my stomach. The vomit rushed out of my mouth as if a bunch of demons were escaping the traps of hell.

"What the fuck is wrong with you?" squelched Larry.

"My lunch must have gotten ruffled when that dude bumped us. Give me a minute."

At that moment, a tall, thin man stepped out of the front door and greeted Larry.

"What's up, playboy?"

"What up, E?" responded Larry.

E was short for Edward Galley, the largest drug dealer east of the Mississippi. He had the eastern shore locked down from D.C. to Miami. Nothing happened past the D.C. border without him knowing about it. The Jamaican Posse conducted business through him when they first came into the area, but later decided they didn't need him and tried to take over the D.C. drug scene. Of course, this caused a war to breakout and E's crew won the war. He had back up from several New York factions, including the Cali Cartel. He had the power and used it to his advantage. I couldn't believe we were able to get that close to him. I knew Jasmine's death was a result of a drug war, but I didn't connect the dots until we'd overheard E's conversation.

"Come on in, my nigga," said E. He then looked at me. "Somebody check this dude."

The guys outside really didn't want to get near me because of the puke, so they just waved me through.

"This is the guy I was telling you about. He's the man who can set up the offshore bank accounts for your loot."

After Larry's introduction, we got into the questioning and answering session about how the operation works. E asked some good questions, which led me to believe that he'd done this type of thing before in the past. Even though I was in the business mode, it took a lot of restraint to not jump across the room and twist his head off. Besides, I knew that if I tried anything, Larry and I wouldn't make it out of the house alive. I remained calm until we got to the negotiations.

"Five points?" exclaimed E. "Nigga, that's highway robbery. I might as well put my money in a secured bank and let the white man fuck me."

"Not only will the white man fuck you, the Feds will too. My service alleviates all of that. Besides, you'll make my fees back in interest after the first month."

"I hear all of that, but the point is that you are trying to fuck me."

"E, this is my business. I am not in the business of fucking people. I take a big risk moving that type of money. If I am caught with it, then I have to explain where the hell it came from."

"So the five points is hush money?"

"No, the five points is the handling fee."

"Okay, here's the deal, Mico," said E as he leaned back and lit a cigarette.

I was shocked that he new my real name. Larry introduced me as Gino because that was the only name I had given him, and Talia knew the rules, so she wouldn't have given up my real name. E was more clever than I expected.

"Caught you by surprise?" asked E. "You didn't think I would give ten million dollars to someone I didn't know, did you? When Larry first told me about you, I had him set up a meeting in public so I could get some nice mug shots."

E tossed a handful of pictures in my lap.

"It wasn't hard finding out who you were."

"So now that you know who I am, we should be able to do business with no problems."

"Exactly what I was thinking, but, with a slight twist."

"What kind of twist?"

"I'm not going to give you five points to handle my money. In fact, I'm tempted not to give you anything because of your dishonesty, but I know you got expenses and there is some risk involved, so I am going to give you twenty five grand to make my money disappear."

"Do you realize that not only will I be making the money disappear, I will also be washing the money for you?"

"And I am sure you will do a good job."

I could have challenged him, but I knew I would lose. He was actually giving me an offer that I wouldn't dare refuse, so I took it in stride. Besides, he was giving me ten million dollars to shuffle for him. I could take as much as I wanted off the top and he would never know it. I let him feed his ego by being the big man but, as always, I knew I would eventually get the last say.

"So, it's a deal?" asked E.

"It's a deal," I replied.

"Man, you're not as shrewd as all the magazines make you out to be. Okay, all transactions will be handled through Larry. He's my mouthpiece on this deal. Understand?"

"Understood."

"Because if something happens to my money, not only will I be looking for you, I'll be looking for Larry, too, big-time basketball star or not."

"Everything is on the up and up, E," said Larry as he swallowed the knot in his throat. "We go way back before all of this, you know that."

"Yeah, I know, but with this type of money, motherfuckers catch amnesia quick and loyalties slip."

E had a right to be concerned about handing over that much money to a stranger. I know I would be.

I left E's place with mixed emotions about the deal and strong emotions about making him pay for Jasmine's death. I briefed Larry on the entire process and we set a date for the pick up. Even though a part me was upset with the fact E thought he could hustle me, another part of me was elated that I would get a chance at taking him out. I didn't quite know how I was going to do it. I just knew it had to be done.

The Art of the Deal

I returned to work on Monday with my game face on as usual. I was in rare form as I attended the last meeting to clinch the David Steiner deal. The deal yielded the company one of the largest commissions in corporate history. It was also a pivotal point in my life because I finally got to meet my idol.

David Steiner was as sharp as I thought he would be. He was a man who knew the art of negotiating, hands down. His strategy wasn't as overbearing as I thought it would be, but calm, laid back, and calculated. I could tell he came to the table prepared and with a plan in mind. He knew what he wanted and what he was willing to accept. The deal turned out to be a win–win situation for everyone involved and I think I left a positive impression on him because when the meeting was over, he gave me his personal business card.

With all the big accounts that I landed for the company, I earned my place at the top. It allowed me to sit pretty and coast for a while. All I really was involved in was the training and introduction of new brokers to the game of slinging other people's money—an art and hustle that I mastered all too well, so well, in fact, that my best friend, DJ, resented me for it. He eventually left the company because he couldn't handle my success. Even though I offered to take him along for the ride, he felt that he shouldn't have to ride the coattails of someone he introduced to the game. Unfortunately, he couldn't separate his personal feelings from our business relationship so our friendship faded.

At first, the loss of his friendship bothered me, but then I thought that if he couldn't accept and celebrate my success then he probably wasn't a true friend. Besides, my father used to tell me that a true friend is someone who would die for you. Out of the handful of acquaintances I dealt with, there was no one I could consider as a true friend.

By day, I became the super successful brother everyone admired and looked up to, but by night, I was a meticulous hustler driven by the adrenaline of the next hustle. The penny hustle such as drug dealing or pimping never appealed to me. To me, that was small-time game. I always went for the big score. I figured if I were to get caught doing anything illegal, it would be for something big, not small-time shit.

The game that Carl introduced me to was lucrative and exciting. Thanks to him, my underground operation was running fluently without a hitch, and I wasn't about to let a punk like E disrupt my operation by putting the squeeze on me. I'd always dealt swiftly with people like him in the past but, this time, it was going to take a little more planning and involvement from others to take him out.

I always did my dirt by my lonely, so involving others went against the grain of what made me so illusive. Unfortunately, I had no choice but to solicit some help this time because E was never alone and was always heavily guarded and armed. If I were to go in blasting, I would be committing suicide. The thought of devising a plan to turn him over to the authorities crossed my mind, but that would also be committing suicide because his reach would extend far beyond any prison bars. He would still be able to touch me. I had to wipe out not only him but the roots of his entire organization. Taking out E and his organization would take a lot of time and strategic planning. The first thing I had to do was get embedded into his psyche and learn his routine of doing business.

E didn't want me to take my handling fees from off the top of his deposits and would usually force me to wait in his office while his accountant went over the statements. He insisted on paying me separately, but after I made the initial deposit of ten million dollars and conducted several other transactions for him, he refused to pay me anything for my services. This went on for about six months.

Although, his demands were time-consuming and costly, I didn't resist because it allowed me to get a closer view into his world. After a while, I knew just about everyone in his crew. I knew their names, daily routines, shift changes, and where they hung out. I also found out that E's father was the root of the organization. I finally had all the information I needed to devise my plan. The only challenge left was coming up with a way to get all the players in one place at the same time and having enough firepower to finish the job.

In between my planning E's demise and handling usual business at the office, Talia and I got married and my mother passed away. With both occasions serving as pivotal points in my life, it was time for me to step away from taking unnecessary risks from underground criminal activities. I had to start concentrating on going totally legit. Talia was ready to take this step as well.

As for my mother, I'd already lost her years ago when my father was killed. Her passing removed a major block in my aorta and blood started flowing to my heart unrestricted, thereby, allowing me to love unconditionally. I didn't attend her funeral. I let my brother take care of all the arrangements even though she named me as the executor of her estate. Her last gesture led me to believe that maybe there was actually some method to her madness. Unfortunately, her tactics used while raising me left wounds too deep to be healed by one gesture of confidence in the end. Her death closed a painful chapter in my life and a new one opened up with Talia and me pledging our eternal love for one another.

Stop Thoughting and Start Thinking

There was one other chapter that had to be closed and, unfortunately, I couldn't just walk away from it. I was too deep into E's organization and he definitely wouldn't let me walk away alive. My plan had to be carried out, but I was missing one critical element—the firepower. I certainly couldn't solicit help from my old crew in Detroit, most of them were either dead, locked up, or incapacitated.

After struggling with this part of the plan for several months, I ran across an old address and number that Jasmine had given me when she left for New York to take care of her sick mother. I found the address in an old wallet while Talia and I were unpacking boxes after we moved into a new house we purchased.

I knew it was a long shot, but I had to see if I could find the older brother that Jasmine said was an enforcer for the Jamaican Posse. I thought that he certainly would be interested in finding out who killed his brother and sister. Convincing him would be easy; the difficult part would be finding him. With the lifestyle that he was involved in, I knew he could have easily been killed or locked up. It was a long shot, but it was another gamble I had to take.

I also knew that, as a unit, the Jamaican Posse didn't exist anymore because they were involved in several bloody wars with several drug factions. In fact, some drug cartels even united against them as well as the alphabet authorities such as the DEA, ATF, and the FBI. I knew it would even be a long shot finding an old Posse member, but I had to take it.

The address took me to a burrow in the Bronx that looked like a war zone and reeked of sour piss. I wasn't scared at all. I refused to be scared of my own people. With my street gear on, I walked among them like I belonged there. The only thing that I was afraid would give me away was my non–New York accent.

I only had the name of Jasmine's older brother, Cantone, and her mother's old address. After searching for streets and house numbers in the New York maze, I finally found a brownstone that appeared to have the right address. As I walked up to brownstone, I felt those butterflies starting to flutter again, but there was no turning back, I had to press forward.

The house appeared to be occupied because there were fresh curtains hanging in the window and a light flickering from a television set in the distance. I knocked on the door and waited. Eventually an older man answered the door and, to my surprise, he had a Jamaican accent.

"Ya mon?"

"Hello," I responded. "Would you happen to know a young lady by the name of Jasmine?"

The old man paused for what seemed to be an eternity before responding.

"Yeah, I know her. She's my niece. What you want from her? She dead now, ya know?"

"Yes, I know. I'm an old boyfriend of hers. Mico's my name."

"Mico?" he asked as he stared into my eyes.

He turned and walked away from the door.

I just stood there not knowing if I should enter, walk away, or stay put. As usual, I assumed the worst, so I went into the defensive and alert mode.

The old man returned with a framed photograph in his hands and handed it to me. It was a picture of Jasmine and me. The tears rushed to my eyes and, for a moment, the world went blank.

"You must have loved her very much. I can see it your eyes."

"Yes," I said wiping the tears away. "I do love her very much."

I convinced him to let me in for a brief moment so that I could discuss why I was there. He allowed me to come in, but we didn't talk until after he showed me her room, which he kept in the same order as when she was alive. It was his shrine to honor her memory.

The old man turned out to be her uncle, the brother of her mother. He moved from Jamaica to help Jasmine take care of her mother and to free up some time for her so that she could live a little. He told me how Jasmine would talk so much about me and that after the writing stopped, she vowed to find and marry me. She found me.

"She used to talk about one of her brothers a lot," I said. "Cantone?"

"I know why," he responded. "Cantone was her eldest brother. He was her protector when she was a little girl. Her death disturbed him, I believe, the most out of all of us."

"Is he still around?"

"He disappeared for a long while after it happened. The boy was torn to pieces that he couldn't be there to protect his younger brother and sister. At first, we thought that he had gone to search for the killers, but he wound up in Jamaica on a sabbatical."

"So is he still in Jamaica?"

"No, he returned and is now serving as a minister at the mission a few blocks up."

Shocked and dismayed at the news of Cantone's conversion, I continued to talk with Jasmine's uncle for a while longer before leaving for the mission. I knew that it was going to be a long shot to get Cantone to help me with my plan, but I traveled too far not to try.

Cantone had just finished one of his sermons when a worker at the mission guided me in his direction. He was draped in religious garments, complete with the rosary and crucifix dangling from his neck. His face was riddled with what appeared to be several battle scars and his hands indicated that he wasn't afraid of hard work.

I introduced myself and he immediately acknowledged that he felt he had known me because Jasmine talked so much about me. He also quickly acknowledged and denounced his past life after I explained why I was there. His calm demeanor solidified his contentions that he was no longer walking on the wrong side of the law or the wrong side of life. He also told me that he had prayed that the culprits who killed his family would repent for their dirty deeds just as he had done. It was almost as if he was blaming himself for what had happened to his sister.

I felt that I had hit a brick wall, but just as I was about to leave, Cantone stopped me.

"Hey, broda," he called.

He scribbled an address on a sheet a paper and gave it to me.

"This is my Cousin Mark's information. Wait one hour before you give him a call. I need to call him first to make sure he knows who you are and why you are calling. He might be interested in your plan."

"Thanks. I owe you one."

"You owe me nothing. Just remember that whatever happens, it won't bring my sister back."

He kissed his crucifix and kneeled as if he was praying for me.

I left Cantone on his knees and wandered around the Bronx for about an hour before trying to contact Mark. I grabbed a cup of coffee at one of the local shops and thought about my approach. I tried contacting him by phone for several hours, but to no avail. It was getting dark and there was no way I was going to try to search for his address in the Bronx. I prided myself on being smart, not crazy. I decided to grab a room and start fresh the next day.

After two days, I finally connected with Mark. He was a thin and hyperactive man with a short attention span and a short fuse. It was as if he were on crack, bouncing around and never finishing a thought or completing a sentence.

It turned out that the reason it took so long for me to get in contact with him was because after receiving a call from Cantone, he went underground to recruit the firepower for the plan. He knew what I wanted and was ready to deliver. Mark's eagerness to participate completed all the elements for my plan and now all I had to do was execute.

The Black Chameleon's Wrath

Back at E's camp, I was able to convince him to allow me to extend my offshore banking services to the rest of the crew, including his father, free of charge. He was open to the idea because he wanted me to deposit all of his crew's money into his account, so he agreed to let me explain how it worked during the next group meeting. He would make sure that his father would be at the meeting as well as Big Mike, the man who led the massacre on the Jamaican Posse, and the rest of his top soldiers. There were two stipulations for the meeting: E would not reveal the location for the meeting beforehand, and I had to be picked up by one of his drivers and taken there blindfolded.

At first, I thought that his trust in me subsided, but I quickly found out that no one knew where the meeting would take place except for E, his father, and Big Mike. Everyone else was to be blindfolded and driven to the location just like me. E was very cautious. Using tactics like this was a testament to why he survived on top for so long. This tactic put a hiccup in my plan, but it was certainly not one that I couldn't overcome.

One of the companies that contributed significantly to my investment portfolio's bottom-line developed software for global tracking devices. I contacted the owner of the company and explained that I was considering pitching his company to some of my top investors and wanted to try their latest technology to ensure we had the right fit. The owner agreed without hesitation and provided me with two tracking devices and a team of engineers to help with the testing.

During one of my visits with E, I secretly attached one of the devices to his car so that we could track where the car had been. We were hoping that the car would be driven to the meeting location several times prior to the meeting, which would help us identify its location.

The results from our monitoring revealed that the car visited one place three times during the week of the meeting. It turned out that the location was a warehouse in Southeast D.C. Since the location was a good possibility, Mark assigned some of his guys to scope out the location so that we could developed our plan based on its layout.

On the morning of the meeting, I received a call indicating that the car would pick me up in five minutes. I attached the tracking device to the inseam of my underwear and waited for the driver. And just as E had said, the driver arrived, blindfolded me, and placed me in the car. The plan was now in full swing and there was no turning back because all communications were cut off between Mark and me. The worse that I thought could happen was Mark's men slipping up and killing me by mistake. I just had to trust that all of our planning would pay off.

It turned out that the warehouse we identified in Southeast D.C. was the place that E selected for the meeting. I recognized the layout from a drawing that one of Mark's crew used during the planning. I was at ease with knowing that all of our pre-planning wasn't in vain. Everyone was thoroughly searched before entering the area where we were going to have the meeting. I didn't know what the format of the meeting would be, the seating arrangements, or when I was to start my presentation. The plan was to wait for forty-five minutes after I arrived at the location before making a move on E. I assumed that I would be the last one to speak at the meeting. I was going to address the group presentation style so I would be standing up when everything popped off.

I was right once again. E wanted to handle other business before turning the meeting over to me; however, I didn't plan on Larry being there. I thought about giving Larry some sort of signal to get out of there, but I didn't know how committed he was to E and the wrong gesture could give me away.

The clock seemed to tick in slow motion as I sat there and listened to all of E's babbling and grandeur. I really didn't want to be sitting down when Mark's crew busted in. I wanted to be visible. I wanted to be standing.

For a while, it seemed as if E would never shut up. I saw his lips moving but couldn't really hear anything come out. It was like I was sitting in a classroom with Charlie Brown, listening to his teacher talk. Then it happened. E gave me the floor.

As soon as I stood up to give my presentation, the door was kicked in and the orders started to fly. Mark's men ordered everyone to put their hands in the air where they could see them. Those who didn't comply fast enough were shot at point blank range. Larry was the first to go, but I couldn't show emotion, I had to stay focused. E didn't know what hit him until Mark threw me a gun. But before E could say one word, I unloaded a round in his stomach and one to Big Mike's head.

I was about to go against my cardinal rule, which was to never stay around and watch a man fall after I shot them. As soon as I pulled the trigger, Mark and his crew started in on the rest of the crew. After the smoke cleared, E was the only one still living.

"What the fuck," gasped E.

"I just want to leave you with a few words before I send your ass to hell," I said as I aimed the pistol at his head.

"Who sent you? What the fuck I do to you?"

"You killed my dreams," I responded as I pulled a picture of Jasmine and me out of my back pocket and held it in front of his face. "You killed my dreams twice."

"Fuck you and your dreams," E responded as he closed his eyes and grimaced from the bullet in his belly.

I released two shots to his head.

We got out of there fast, unnoticed, and without a trace. The plan went like clockwork. After we met back at our rendezvous location, I paid Mark and his crew one million dollars as I promised and they disappeared, while I slipped back into my nine-to-five life with my beautiful wife.

Thanks to E's involuntary investment, I was able to purchase a popular hotel and casino on the Las Vegas strip. Many years have passed since my last encounter with the dark side, the side of me that I hope never to see again, but one that I could easily tap into if needed. Talia and I now have three wonderful kids who have everything they could ever want in life and hopefully will never have to resort to some of the things that I had to.

The ribbon-cutting ceremony will happen soon to celebrate the opening of my new casino and to honor my accomplishments. Dignitaries will bestow honors upon me that are fit for a king. The mayor will give me the key to the city and the NAACP will honor me for my cultural connection and significant donations that I have made to their cause over the years. I wonder if they would still honor me if they knew what it really took for me to get to this point in my life.

I don't have any regrets or make any excuses about my journey. I used every ounce of my soul to cope with life's challenges and met every one of them on every front, in the hood and in the boardroom. I took the body shots and the hand that life dealt me and emerged a winner in a society that wasn't built by me or for me. And, just as a chameleon changes its color to adapt to its environment, I changed the color of my character to adapt to mine.

Printed in the United States
45185LVS00003B/1-102